Why Gold? Why Now?

The War Against Your Wealth and How to Win It

E.B. Tucker

Library of Congress Catalog-in-Publication Data is Available:

ISBN: 978-1-7351048-1-2 (paperback)

ISBN: 978-1-7351048-0-5 (ebook)

ISBN: 978-1-7351048-2-9 (paperback – limited edition)

Author: E.B. Tucker

Editor: John Pangere

Front cover image and book design: Fadi Sheikh-Khalil Garcia

Any references to historical events, real people, or real places are recounted by the author on a best effort basis.

First printing edition 2020

Midas Capital Partners, LLC

P.O. Box 23741

Tampa, FL 33623

Disclaimer:

While the author has made every effort to provide accurate data and information in the preparation of this book, neither the publisher nor the author assumes any responsibility for errors or for changes that occur after publication. The information referenced is believed to be reliable, accurate and appropriate, but is not guaranteed in any way. The strategies and forecasts herein are the author's sole opinion and could prove to be inaccurate. No company, individual, or entity compensated the author or publisher for mention in this book.

This book contains the specific names of companies, strategies, types and sizes of physical gold, none of which can be deemed recommendations to readers of the book. Purchasing and reading this book does not constitute a fiduciary relationship. Data, company specific or otherwise, will not be updated on an ongoing basis. After publication, the author and publisher will not be responsible for future developments.

A registered financial advisor is always the best source of guidance in making financial decisions. The author is not a registered financial advisor and does not address the individual financial condition of readers of this book.

The author is a director and significant shareholder of Metalla Royalty & Streaming, a royalty firm mentioned in this book. This book contains "forward-looking information" and "forward-looking statements" within the meaning of applicable Canadian and U.S. securities legislation. The forward-looking statements herein are made as of the date of update only, and the author does not assume any obligation to update or revise them. Forward-looking statements and information include, but are not limited to, statements with respect to the future price of gold and other commodities, the possibility of a monetary crisis, potential economic contractions, potential for increasing public debt, the positioning of Metalla and their ability to capitalize on current and future market conditions, the ability for Metalla to grow through accretive transactions in the future, the future value of Metalla's portfolio of assets, the value of Metalla in relation to possible increases in the price of gold, competitive uncertainties, and contingencies. Forward-looking statements and information are subject to various known and unknown risks and uncertainties, many of which are beyond the ability of the author, publisher, or Metalla to control or predict, that may cause actual results, performance or achievements to be materially different from those expressed or implied thereby, and are developed based on assumptions about such risks, uncertainties, and other factors set out herein. No forward-looking statement can be guaranteed, and actual future results may vary materially. Accordingly, readers are advised not to place undue reliance on forward-looking statements or information.

Written in just 23 days, this book would not be possible without the help of:

My righthand man John Pangere

and

My sister Leigh Tucker

I am grateful for you both.

"A blind person does not know what darkness is.

They have never seen light to compare it to darkness."

Alan Watts *Out of Your Mind*

Table of Contents

Introduction – The Golden Path

This is a self-defense book. It's your wealth that needs defending.

If you work, save, sacrifice or strive for something better, you're building wealth. It takes time. You go without. You delay gratification today for a better tomorrow.

Then in one quick instant the rules of the game change. The value of money changes. Nobody consults you, the one who chose discipline yesterday for a better tomorrow.

I (E.B. Tucker) want to share with you the most important single piece of financial insight I have. The role of gold is set to take on a meaning not one in a thousand sees today.

If you don't know about gold, don't worry. If you have preconceived notions about gold, let them go.

This book may be your best resource for surviving what's on the horizon. It could radically change the course of your life going forward. It may mean avoiding unnecessary hardship. Better yet, it could mean capitalizing on events others don't see coming.

To do this well we'll need to answer two questions. First, why gold?

We'll go through a brief history of the yellow metal. We'll see why some people call it "the money of kings." We'll look back at why it once underpinned our financial system. We'll see how politicians and governments can't resist the temptation to spend tomorrow's hard-earned income today.

This is nothing new. We'll look at how recent history matches ancient history. We'll see how gold always tells the truth about government money. It exposes all the tricks played by government spendthrifts and political grifters.

However, don't expect a dry lecture in the pages ahead. We - you and I - may at times gloss over an entire decade in a page or two. This book is not a doctoral thesis, it's your handbook for surviving the turbulent future of what we call money.

That's why the other question we'll answer is, Second: why now?

Problems with money start slowly, then escalate quickly, almost in an instant. If you pay attention to the signs, you see what's coming. You have plenty of time to prepare. But most people don't. It's not over their heads, they just don't want to look. They leave it to the "experts" who created the problem in the first place.

We'll see how aberrations in the U.S. money system began in the mid-20th century. There were flare ups, but most people blamed those on outside factors, enemy nations or other circumstances. Those weren't one-time events, they were clues.

Bailouts, common today, started small. Just a few billion dollars to help Mexico in 1995 or unwind an over-leveraged hedge fund betting on currencies in 1998. These bailouts of the past pale in comparison to those of today.

In 2020, the pace of already-bloated federal deficit spending nearly doubled before summer. I'll share with you my prediction of the shocking next step ahead on this dangerous road.

When we're finished, you'll know why gold matters, and how to own it. You'll know how to buy gold in physical form, on the stock exchange, or through owning the shares of companies that produce it.

I'll go one step further and share what I believe is the best way to own gold. It doesn't involve mining, or worse, betting on the next scoundrel who promises to "find gold" using your money as seed capital. Both are tough businesses. I have years of experience with them, so I'll share plenty of first-hand examples.

Instead, I prefer shares of gold royalty companies, one of them specifically. Royalties claim a small percentage of the gold produced over the life of a mine. They don't get involved in actual mining. Today I sit on the board of one such company. I'll share that company's philosophy which I helped shape.

This is your practical guide to the world of gold. The history, fundamentals and insights of the past are just trivia fodder if we don't know how to use them to our advantage. Once the inevitable happens, it's too late to prepare. Right now, there's still time.

I want a financial novice or a seasoned investor to walk away from this book with the same feeling. There has not been a more urgent time to understand the role of gold and how to own it.

Why I Wrote This Book

The price of gold is on the rise. So is its importance.

Many of my friends who after learning why gold is so important couldn't figure out how to buy it. Worse yet, those with financial advisors often met fierce resistance.

Gold has a track record dating back thousands of years. Kings, countries and barbarians all counted on it to store wealth when under ultimate pressure. After a decade of watching the stock market rise, I'm not sure the average financial advisor today knows what real pressure is.

That's why these advisors, and even my friends, think gold is too complex. They write it off as expensive, risky, or not worth the effort. In fact, just the opposite is true.

Gold is simple. It's the only asset that doesn't depend on something else for its value. Stocks depend on a company's profits, bonds on a coupon payment, apartments need tenants. Gold needs nothing. It's pure, unadulterated wealth.

That's exactly why governments hate it. Gold tells the truth about value. It exposes games that governments play with the value of money. We'll go through many examples.

However, before we begin, it's important for you to understand why my thoughts on gold are worth your time. After all, everything you read in these pages is just my conclusion after years of studying gold.

Informed opinions matter in financial markets. They show you a future most people can't envision. If you wait for hard, fast proof in any investment it's too late.

To get a major market move right, like the one I see ahead for gold, it takes two things. The first piece is a little imagination. That doesn't mean grandiose daydreaming. It means quiet study and contemplation to get an accurate take on where we are. Then it's possible to see where we're going. I'll show you how to back away and see what the masses can't.

The second piece is the knowledgebase needed to understand what you see once you back away. Your first look doesn't help much because there's nothing to compare it to. It takes years of wins, losses, and near misses to build up the experience needed to recognize opportunity. I'll share mine with you as we go along. I won't hold anything back.

I'll share how I first learned about gold in 2000 when it traded for $275/oz. I didn't buy it. I'll tell you why I waited more than four more years to buy my first ounce.

More importantly I'll share how my interest in gold grew as I lived and worked through a decade of excessive credit. Things didn't look right to me, and they weren't.

How I Got Here

I discovered gold was a store of wealth for the world's most iconic families. I met some of them. I asked them questions I know you'd want to know the answers to.

A few years into my journey, let's call that journey "the golden path," my employer wisely fired me from a sales position. Sitting in the office talking about gold and gold stocks on the phone all day somehow irritated them.

Unemployed, my closest friends in finance urged me to write a blog. They even set up a website for me. My suspicion now is they were worn out from receiving lengthy mass-emails with my take on state of all things financial and philosophical.

Writing helped me solidify my take on things. It's a serious craft. It's one thing to spout off ideas at a neighborhood barbecue. It's another to put them in print, as I'll do here.

At some stage on the golden path I realized my journey was not about money. I was enamored with economics, philosophy and using the two to predict what people and markets would do next. My most successful investment bets incorporated these elements. Once I knew that, I made it my sole mission to learn every possible tool that would help me refine my thinking.

That helped me narrowly avoid the brunt of the 2008 stock market crash. An early September 2008 sale of my largest stock holding, Lincoln National Corp (LNC), at $55/share gave me what I considered to be a windfall. When the stock fell to $5/share within weeks of my sale, I knew I dodged a bullet.

I had met the company's CEO at its annual shareholder meeting three years earlier. Nobody goes to annual meetings typically. I do. You get to shake hands with the executives. This one in particular had a weak handshake. I never forgot it.

To be clear, my stock sale at $55/share before it tumbled to $5/share weeks later was mostly luck. However, anyone who frequently experiences good luck will tell you hard work improves your odds.

I saw this small windfall as my chance to turn luck into opportunity. I had already established intellectual independence. I wanted financial independence.

In November 2008, realizing this was likely my one chance to elevate myself quickly, I put that windfall to work. I bought gold at $720/oz, silver at $9/oz, several dividend-paying exchange-traded funds (ETFs), and more LNC shares than I sold previously paying on average $9/share for it this time.

Then the price of everything surged. By the next summer I had about triple what I started with. Again, this was catching the market at an extreme bottom. Most people were afraid to buy stocks. Others were bankrupt. 2009 was a tough year all around.

But it's important you understand I wasn't working with a giant sum of money. I didn't have a safety net.

In 2009 I was a divorced bachelor living in a small house I could only afford with a roommate. Don't get me wrong, I wasn't poor, but I was well aware of how serious the stakes were. And the thought of going back to work for a company was a nightmare.

A Perspective on the 2008 Bust Many Missed

The 2008 bust created what I saw as the opportunity of a lifetime to buy rental property.

With my trading windfall in hand, I set out to buy rental houses figuring everyone facing foreclosure would rent for a decade. More demand for rentals meant improving economics for landlords. That's what you want to see when you make an investment.

I built a spreadsheet to compute what I felt would be a can't-lose offer price. This was the second half of 2009. I was too early, which frustrated me. I must have made 100 offers before one hit.

Then, in early 2010, they hit so fast I ran out of capital by summer. I now had a small portfolio of single-family rental houses. Since I paid cash, I owned them outright. I organized all of the repair work myself. I also leased them myself for the first few years. Thanks to discipline with my offers and hard work, I parlayed a modest windfall into a self-sufficient stream of rental income.

With what I felt was ultimate freedom (those were the days!) I spent all of my time studying the one investment that mystified me.

During my late-2008 stock buying spree I also picked up some gold mining stocks. I already understood the basics of gold, it's place in my financial life, and how to own it. But mining stocks were new.

Some of the mining stocks I bought rose in value by about 500%, give or take. I felt like a genius. Then in the years that followed they largely crashed, almost back to where I bought them. I felt like an idiot. I had to know how this happened.

In early 2011 my good friend Dick Coley gave a piece of advice that changed the course of my professional and financial life. He's a smart guy, Harvard graduate, successful real estate developer, and generally wise man. In his early 60s at the time, he liked my enthusiasm.

I told Dick I didn't enjoy tending to my real estate. Don't get me wrong, I didn't want to sell it (I still hold it today), but it was boring. This wasn't about money, it was about stimulation.

He asked me what I liked doing most. Without hesitation I said studying gold, gold stocks, and what makes them tick. He said, "Do more of that and hire someone to manage your property." I asked how I'd earn enough money to make a business out of this. He told me, "Don't worry about it."

Dick was so right I could have paid him $1 million for that advice. I've told him a dozen times how much it helped me, and he admits he barely remembers our chat.

I went home and booked a trip to New York to attend a one-day hard asset conference on gold. Sitting in the front row, which I think is the essential way to get the most out of any lecture, I met Brett Heath.

Today, Brett is the CEO of the fastest-growing gold royalty company by stock price. I am on the board of directors. More on that later. Before reaching that peak, we walked through a big valley.

Brett read my blog articles when he returned home to California. We talked on the phone a few times, then more frequently. I went to visit. We had a complementary chemistry. I wrote articles, pitched my ideas, and generally pestered people into a back and forth on gold that sharpened my views. Brett sat back, quiet, studying everything. We made an interesting combination.

After a few months he called me with a wild idea. He was in the airport boarding a plane to Argentina. A new friend we met at another gold conference offered the chance to meet Doug Casey, who in our view was a philosophical icon in the gold world. (Years later I'd write Doug's eponymous newsletter. I'd also coax him into investing in our royalty company day one, which turned out to be a big win.)

On the way to the connecting flight Brett pitched the idea of starting a financial advisory firm focused exclusively on gold and silver stocks. I'd handle the communications with clients and prospects. He'd study the companies. We'd share responsibility for trading.

We did it, and it was a grind. We visited dozens of mining sites and prospective properties. We attended conferences. Tight on funds, we'd always share a room, often far from the action to avoid inflated prices. To say we had a limited budget was an understatement.

In the end, we struggled. We raised millions of dollars, but it takes hundreds of millions to make it as a fund. The problem wasn't a lack of effort. If there was a duo who knew gold better than we did, we didn't meet them.

We'd meet with hedge fund managers, asset advisors, family offices, and other institutional investors who'd tell us they'd never had a meeting where they learned more. We'd show them rocks from mines, photos, video of controlled explosions on site, pictures of us in dump trucks, next to smelters, holding bars of gold...we did it all. But we couldn't fight a falling gold market.

From the day I first felt a spark for gold in 2000 to the time we had the fund operational, gold ran from a low of $254/oz to $1,921/oz. As this chart shows, after hitting an all-time high in 2011, gold fell for four years straight.

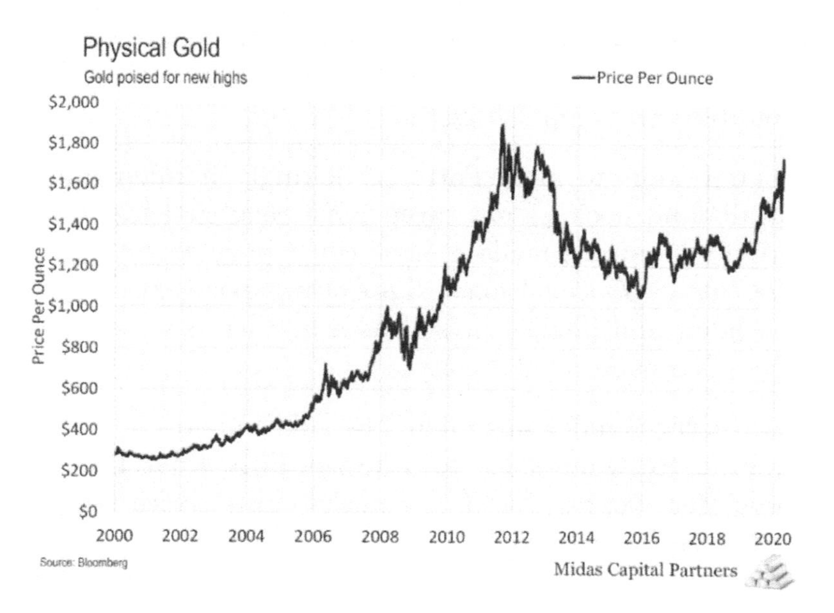

In early 2013 I told Brett we needed to close the fund, returning shares to our investors. Years later, most of the companies we owned were snapped up by rivals at a premium. Others surged on to success independently. We felt like we did the best we could for our investors who trusted us with a portion of their wealth.

As for us, two wayward goldbugs, it was the end of the line. The decision to close down wasn't easy. In fact, we didn't fully agree on it. Brett was hesitant. I insisted.

An Unlikely Diversion

Officially out of work, I was ready for something stable. Fighting a falling gold price for a few years really takes its toll. What I later learned was nothing teaches you about cycles like fighting one. The merciless beating wears you out and helps straighten out your thinking.

While running the fund, a local friend sent some of my blog entries to a newsletter writer named Porter Stansberry.

He posted them on his website and appreciated the free content. I decided to check in with him and see if there was something we could do together.

When I went to meet Porter, I jokingly handed him a spiralbound book of my three most-read articles. I say jokingly because I made a mock cover page with the title *The Heretic Letter.* I made light of my experiences up to this point and pitched myself as a guy who's so early he disrupts conventional society.

Stansberry found it so amusing he asked me to come work for him. He wanted me to do essentially what I'd been doing for years, research stocks and write stories explaining why I liked them. I had no idea he ran the largest paid retail newsletter service in the world. He assured me if things didn't work out, we'd part ways as friends. Turns out, it was a fun job. It helped that I was well-prepared for it.

Over time I discovered that the newsletter business is a marketing business masquerading as a financial research firm. However, someone has to write the actual research. It needs to be decent, or people cancel. It was my job to produce accurate market calls. What the dozens of marketers did with it from there didn't concern me. After all, I'd done the same thing for years often earning far less.

I covered the types of companies I knew. There were rental housing firms going public, insurance companies I thought had problems, and of course, there was gold.

In late 2013 I recommended an early-stage gold exploration and development company sitting on a monster gold hoard. I knew a hedge fund owned more than 10% of the stock and announced it would shut down. That meant it had to sell the stock quickly. We got in for $2/sh.

In the spring of 2020 that stock traded for $12/share, 500% higher than my recommendation, far outpacing the rising gold price.

I had a different perspective and that turned out to be a needed asset. Eventually, I went on to write other premium newsletters at Stansberry. The company charged high prices for these products. I tried to make them as good as possible by pouring myself into the work. I've looked into about every type of business you can imagine.

I met a lot of interesting people along the way. I helped launch famed author and newsletter writer Bill Bonner's new publication the *Bill Bonner Letter*. We wrote together for a year traveling around the world between his nine homes. Central France, remote northwestern Argentina, Baltimore, Maryland...we covered a big swath of the globe telling stories others couldn't or wouldn't. At the heart of it we tried to help people question their economic premises. Some did.

Then in 2015 I flew to Aspen, Colorado, to meet with Doug Casey near his ranch home. This was a long way from the days of standing in a line at gold conferences to shake his hand.

We sorted out how I'd take over his monthly newsletter. Doug's classic work and *New York Times* bestseller *Crisis Investing* in 1980 launched him into iconic fame in the gold newsletter world. He's a speculator, intellectual and, at his core, one of the most thoughtful and interesting people you'll ever meet.

Doug understood my background. When I called him up in November of the following year, he trusted me on what seemed like a big risk. I told him my longtime friend and business partner Brett was about to take his tiny company public. Brett would use stock to buy gold royalties that fit his model. He had 100 potential targets defined and felt he could double that. I told Doug that, in addition to making a significant investment, I'd join the board to personally watch over things.

MTA Director Lawrence Roulston (left) MTA CEO Brett Heath (center) Author (right)

Just over three years later in early 2020 that stock began trading on the New York Stock Exchange. I still serve on its board of directors. The company is Metalla Royalty & Steaming (MTA).

Why I'm Sharing This

Please know, this is not a chest-pounding exercise. I want to show you that my path became "the golden path" by working, learning, risking and being willing to abandon the mold of what professional life should look like. I took risks with my career that I can't in good conscience advise others to take.

The result is a knowledge base that sets me up with a big responsibility. I must write this book for the average investor, any person with a dollar of savings. It's the average investor who needs to understand the looming threats to what we call money -- then to see that gold, the money of kings, is a refuge for wealth.

Many people think gold is a safe-haven asset. That's true to some degree, but it's far more than that.

A rising gold price can lead to immense profits for those properly positioned. I'll show you what I believe will be the best, and the most important, investment I'll make in my entire financial career.

At the end of this book I hope you'll see the world from a different perspective. I hope that perspective helps you navigate what's ahead with an insight you didn't have before investing this time with me.

Now, enough about me and how I ended up here, let's get to why gold is the most important investment today.

Part I – Why Gold?

Chapter 1 – Human Nature Is the Problem

The first quarter of 2020 marked the end of capitalism as we know it. That's what the history books will say.

Within one three-month period, we saw an all-time high for stocks, a 34% decline – the fastest on record – and an economic lockdown stopping the economy in its tracks. There is no precedent for this type of volatile action.

It's only possible in an economic system warped by bad incentives. Let me explain.

Most people fixate on what just happened and miss the big picture. Think of a fiery couple who sees a counselor each week shouting over each other to lay blame for the most recent tiff. A good counselor points out it's not this week's fight, it's the whole relationship. What you would call a systemic problem.

What's wrong with the U.S. money system is systemic. The most recent bailout doesn't matter. The next bailout doesn't matter. It's the system of incentives in place to meet every problem with an ever-greater pile of borrowed money. The longer that goes on, the bigger and more dramatic the problems become.

To get the big picture right we need to see the pattern. Then it's easy to see what's next. What's next is more of the same until the system as we know it breaks. When that day comes, it will be too late to seek protection. Someone will be left holding the bag. It doesn't have to be you.

I remember late September 2008. The headlines said U.S. Treasury Secretary Hank Paulson dropped to his knees begging Speaker of the House Nancy Pelosi for a $700 billion bailout. Without the bailout politicians and bankers said the world as we knew it would implode.

Fast forward to March 2020. Within five weeks of the all-time high in stocks politicians and bankers said without an urgent $2.2 trillion bailout the world as we knew it would implode. They added another nearly a half-trillion dollars the following month. That short time alone nearly doubled the annual federal budget. They borrowed every cent from the future.

Between those two events we had unprecedented Federal Reserve involvement in markets. It bought trillions of dollars of treasury bonds, mortgage bonds and other debt securities in an attempt to control interest rates.

If the Federal Reserve tried to fix the price of coffee beans or corn, there would be an uproar. Somehow when it comes to the cost of money it gets a pass. It's rare to find someone who handles that kind of power responsibly. More likely, a feeling of omnipotence sets in. When that happens, watch out.

The temptation that comes with the power to create money is irresistible. People in power today just can't help themselves.

To politicians, a recession means being blamed and losing reelection. To bankers and the most connected money men, a recession means facing big losses on bad financial bets. These two groups share the same incentive to prop up the economy. They also have the power to help each other prevent pain.

The only thing that changed between 2008 and 2020 was the size of the bailout. The numbers never get smaller. The bailouts and special loans are always temporary. The problem is, nobody wants to endure the hard work of repayment later.

Worldwide stimulus packages topped $12 trillion in the first half of 2020. That's 13% of world Gross Domestic Product (GDP) which stood at around $90 trillion at the time. That's the value of all goods and services produced.

To put this in simple terms, imagine you earn $100,000 per year. Something happens and your income declines 10%, maybe more. So, you rush to borrow $13,000 hoping to cushion the blow. On the surface that sounds fine. After all, you've got to eat and keep the lights on.

Here's the problem. The borrowed money didn't further your education, which would boost earning power. It didn't buy a piece of equipment you'd use to earn more. Instead, it went to rent payments, beer, and pizza. You borrowed to make sure your lifestyle didn't change when your income did.

We all know that doesn't work. We also know that first $13,000 loan wouldn't be the last. When that ran out there'd be another, and another. The loans would grow as long as someone stood by ready to lend.

The recent trillions of dollars in emergency bailout money went to buy pizza and beer for lots of people. In the U.S. around 10-15% went out as a direct payment to lower-income tax filers. Six-figure earners got nothing. The balance bailed out junk-rated companies, over-indebted businesses that would otherwise be insolvent in the face of a tiny economic slowdown.

The $12 trillion already spent around the world will never see repayment. It will end up on the top of a heaping mound of accumulated debts closing in on $300 trillion by the end of 2020.

Where Gold Comes in

The value of all the gold in the world was just under $10 trillion in March 2020. That's every ounce held in vaults, safe deposit boxes, jewelry cases, and even in people's mouths as shiny fake teeth.

Compare that to the $12 trillion that already-broke governments borrowed to pump into their fragile economies. That only took days. Mining the world's $10 trillion worth of gold took thousands of years.

Governments can create limitless amounts of money. Politicians think every sign of pain deserves a bailout. They've done it for years. The pace and scale only increase. They'll never stop.

Gold on the other hand doesn't answer to any decree. Politicians can take it away from people, which we'll discuss later. But they can't order an increase in production. It's just not possible.

That makes gold a store of wealth. While worldwide debt grows at record pace, the supply of gold grows at around 1.5% per year.

According to The World Gold Council, the total above-ground gold supply was 190,000 metric tons at the end of 2017. That's the estimated total of all the gold ever mined up to that point.

While it sounds like a lot, it's much less than you think. All the gold mined in human history would barely fill three Olympic swimming pools.

The supply grows slowly because gold is difficult to produce. First, you've got to find it. Then figure out how to get it out of the earth. Then hire a small army of miners to make this all happen. We're talking about huge risks.

Compare the toil and sweat required to increase the gold supply with the ease of boosting government spending. There's no comparison.

According to the average Congressman, borrowing and spending a few trillion dollars here and there is the only thing that will keep the economy moving. The problem is this money ends up wasted. Nobody respects an unearned dollar. All that's left is a larger pile of debt than before.

Gold is the antidote to this problem with the human condition. Gold has integrity, modern money does not. Gold is money.

Chapter 2 – The Definition of Money

To be called money, a monetary instrument needs to satisfy three requirements.

First, it has to function as a medium of exchange. This means people will readily accept it as payment for goods and services. Governments can help bolster the case for their respective money. The IRS for instance will only accept U.S. Federal Reserve Notes (that's the actual name for the dollar) as tax payment.

Second, it must be a unit of account. There was a time when tobacco and other crops backed money. However, variables like weather and a bad growing season change crop yields and alter supply. The value of something called money needs to be predictable.

Third, it must be a store of value. Here's where we have a problem. To be money, a currency needs to give workers the ability to save it confidently. That savings turns into capital fueling investment and growth. The quantity and integrity of our money today is in question. When trillions of dollars appear at the click of a button, there's no incentive to build savings.

Keep in mind, gold functions well as money because it's hard to create. Its supply grows slowly. Central banks and governments don't like that. Savers do.

The U.S. Federal Reserve, which is incidentally not federal and not a reserve, publishes plenty of papers and interviews with representatives talking about money. You can even visit the St. Louis branch of the Fed to see a cube of $1 million worth of $1-dollar bills, an amount of money which was once a real fortune.

1 million $1 bills – St. Louis Fed

A long time ago I started to worry that the Fed wasn't a good steward of my dollars. It's fair to say "my dollars" because I amassed them in spending less than I earned. Meanwhile, the Fed helped the U.S. government do the opposite.

To be fair, government finance does not work the way a small business does.

You've probably heard friends and neighbors say the government "prints money" or "it will go bust." While they have a point, these theories are not technically true.

Governments Can't Exactly Go Bankrupt

Several years ago, I had the chance to meet a famous economist named Warren Mosler. He founded a firm called Illinois Income Investors in the early 1980s. Under his leadership the firm posted some of the hedge fund industry's most impressive and consistent results.

Mosler is a genius. He tinkers with cars, boats, engines. When I say "tinker" I mean he starts a company that attempts radical innovations with each. He lives high atop a hill in St. Croix, U.S. Virgin Islands. While there on business, I met his tennis partner at a local lawyer's office. He kindly offered to set up the meeting.

Over breakfast, Mosler made a statement that most people won't understand. He said the government can essentially create an unlimited amount of money. Of course, he didn't mean a helicopter would drop $2 billion on every house in suburbia.

More practically, deficits don't matter because the nation only goes bankrupt if nobody accepts its currency. Since people, businesses, and trading partners have to take U.S. currency, the government has a lot of rope to work with.

Mosler is right. In a sense, the debt doesn't matter. A government doesn't function the way a small business does. When it comes to money and debt, the system is more complex. It has different variables.

That doesn't mean endless spending is free of consequence. Eventually the numbers get too big. The debt load can crush the economic engine supporting it.

Years ago, I wrote U.S. debt doubles under each eight-year president going back to Reagan. It's roughly true. Clinton slightly missed the double. Obama made up the slack. On average, you can count on the debt doubling during an eight-year term of any modern U.S. president.

When Trump took office in 2016, debt stood at a little less than $19 trillion. I predicted it would double over the next eight years, which seemed impossible at the time. Three years in, it's over $25 trillion. It's climbing faster today than ever before. I have no doubt it will hit $38 trillion, a full double, by 2024.

Without natural restraint the numbers get exponential. Trillions, quadrillions, quintillions, soon we'll need new words to quantify the debt burden.

Meanwhile, the economic engine supporting that debt shrinks under the weight of the growing debt burden. It needs more tax revenue to pay interest on the ballooning debt. Promises to voters overwhelm revenues flowing in from shrinking tax receipts. Everything becomes sluggish, overburdened, and eventually doesn't work at all.

Again, we're not worried about the U.S. going bankrupt. Governments have the power to tax, incentivize and compel behavior. The next time your friends talk about government finances, you'll have the facts on your side.

What worries us today is protecting our hard-earned wealth from the government's next move.

Wealth Insurance

Wealth isn't something only billionaires need to consider. It's what's left over when you spend less than you earn. It's capital. It's the tangible result of hard work and sacrifice. That wealth is in serious trouble. Gold is the antidote.

Gold is wealth insurance. It can't be produced in unlimited quantity like government money. However, most people aren't interested in wealth insurance today. They're caught up in the day-to-day noise that clutters a non-thinking mind. They miss the big picture. They miss the warning signs.

It's a lot like hurricane insurance. Nobody wants to buy it before the storm. After the storm levels a community, everyone wants it and insurance companies don't want to sell it. The irony is, after the storm passes, there probably won't be another one for years.

Worse yet, hurricane insurance rates jump after the storm. A wise man buys the insurance before the storm, when it's cheap.

Wealth insurance is cheap today. Meanwhile, the threats to wealth have never been greater. Just like a community where no one remembers the last storm doesn't see the point in storm insurance, nobody wants gold today. That will change.

Once wealth is in serious trouble, obvious trouble, we'll see a surge in demand for gold. It's too late to get positioned once that happens.

This is how markets work. They lull you into submission. People tell you there hasn't been a storm for years. What's the use in having that insurance? Stop paying it. Better yet, spend the money and enjoy yourself.

This is where it's important to understand the big picture. I'm talking about seeing the big market cycles. They ebb and flow over longer periods of time. When you look, it's obvious. Most people think it's too complicated. The truth is, they're unwilling to look.

What's truly complicated is losing a chunk of your wealth every 8-10 years in a market crisis. If you notice, the average person is a defenseless sheep when these strike. It doesn't have to be that way.

Think back to the dot-com boom, the housing bust, and the late stages of the stock market rally that ended in early 2020. Each one of these slowly sucked in everyone watching. First the smart money, then astute investors, then the surging masses. Finally, even the naysayers.

This is how a big market trend works. It eventually wears out even the loudest skeptics. It draws in doubters. One by one it takes in everyone. When there's no one left, it changes direction -- usually turning on a dime, wiping out wealth almost overnight.

Believe it or not, this will happen with gold in the coming years.

Right now, strong hands hold gold. That means gold sits in the vaults, bank boxes, home safes, and private bank accounts of very sound thinkers. They don't speculate. They hold gold as wealth insurance.

They see what's ahead for the fragile money system. There's never been a more important time to own its purest antidote. It's not too late for average investors to do the same.

There's a trick to getting off the beach before the tidal wave. I'll share it with you. I'll even do you one better. I'll show you how to see the tidal wave building, surf it, and still have the chance to get off before it wipes out the village.

In the coming years, the radical government money experiments of the 20th century will explode like land mines. Gold will prove the only viable protection from unconstrained politicians and their co-conspirators, the central banks.

As the tally of world debt climbs towards and past $300 trillion, we'll see the merits of gold on full display.

In the coming pages we'll go into a brief history of gold, just the key points. It's important we understand why gold protects wealth. Then, we'll get into how to own it.

Chapter 3 – Sound Money Is the Solution

The sound of two gold coins colliding is unmistakable. There's nothing else like it.

Coin dealers will often strike one gold coin with another to avoid buying a fake. They call this the ping test.

The same goes for silver. Both are precious metals. They have similar physical properties.

If you have two gold or silver coins, try it for yourself. Balance the coin you want to test on your index finger. Hold the coin you know is real in your other hand. Gently tap the coin balanced on your index finger. Listen to the sound.

If both coins are authentic precious metal, you'll hear what sounds like the noise a tuning fork makes. It's deep. It resonates. It's a sound that's very difficult to fake.

Now try the same with two modern quarters or other recently minted coins. Those modern coins contain cheaper metals like zinc and tin. Striking them produces a clink sound that disappears almost instantly.

The ping test to identify sound money has been around for a long time. Roman soldiers used it 2,000 years ago to verify payment after returning from battle.

This is where the term sound money comes from. Sound money was a major concern as the empire grew. Soldiers didn't want to risk their lives for coins made of bronze or other cheaper metals.

The Romans had money problems. Not at first, but over time the empire spent far more than it earned. In order to hold on to power various emperors cheapened the currency.

Currency Debasement

Take the denarius for example. This was a common coin that had several iterations over the course of the Roman Empire.

The first strike of the denarius coin (meaning the version introduced into circulation) had a specific weight which created certainty between trading partners. The coins were consistent. The denarius met the definition of money initially. That didn't last.

In 211 BC the denarius coin contained more than 95% silver. Just 11 years later in 200 BC the Romans cheapened the coin. They shrunk the coin by 14% while keeping the silver percentage content the same.

There are two ways to cheapen government money in coin form. One is to shrink the coin. This allows them to say they didn't remove any silver content, which is true. Only the size of the coin shrinks which means less silver in each coin.

The second trick is reducing silver altogether. Silver is expensive. Replacing it with cheaper metals means the coin looks the same to the untrained eye. It takes people time to notice the change and revalue the cheaper coin. This was a popular tactic for Roman emperors.

As the empire swelled, expenses followed. In 64 AD under Nero's rule, the coin shrunk by another 13%. At the same time, silver content fell by 3%.

Governments can't help themselves when it comes to devaluing money. It was true 2,000 years ago. It's true today. The means don't change, only the methods.

The Romans initially shrunk the size of the coin to help shore up confidence in their money. The lower silver content made the coins cheaper to produce. That allowed Rome to increase the supply of the coins. It bought the empire more time. These types of money games never last. Another devaluation always follows.

Eventually, the emperor Aurelian took silver out almost entirely. This is an outright debasing of the currency.

Debasement in money terms means radically reducing the value of the coin. Roman currency debasement was constant with silver content falling to 83% around 150 AD, 48% around 241 AD, and finally to 5% in 274 AD.

By the later stages of the western Roman Empire, the denarius was worthless. It shows how long this process can go on.

Governments have weapons. They can mandate acceptance of currency, worthless or otherwise. Citizens have few options as long as the government maintains power. However, this can't last forever.

Citizens begin to scramble once they notice. They start storing wealth outside the government's official money system.

Throughout history gold is the easiest way to do it. It's untraceable. It's easily recognizable. It's readily accepted.

It doesn't decay over time. Most importantly, there's no way for governments to debase it. That's why they don't want you to own it.

In the summer of 2019 I spoke at a gold mining conference in London. I stayed for a few extra days to take meetings around town. One of them put a spotlight on how close we are to another devaluation in today's money system.

Wise Words in a Mayfair Basement

A Norwegian friend of mine arranged a meeting with a discrete former Swiss banker he was sure I'd find interesting. He sent me an address in Mayfair. If you're not familiar with London, it's the part of town where all the hedge funds and family offices set up shop.

A receptionist escorted me to an elevator and down to a basement conference room where she told me to wait for my host.

When he arrived, we talked for several hours about the state of things. We covered the money system, the cracks we both noticed, and what's next.

At twice my age this man led two Swiss banks through the 1970s and 1980s. He served as director on numerous well-known public company boards including major banking and energy companies. He understands how money flows through the world. He also understands the value of gold. That's why my Norwegian friend insisted we meet.

He asked me if I know the true value of the U.S. dollar. In his words, "The value of the dollar today is a dozen nuclear-powered aircraft carrier battle groups." What he meant was, you take the money as payment, or else.

That's eerily similar to what the Romans had. By the 3rd and 4th century soldiers took the bronze coins as payment or faced consequences. Consequences only work for so long. Eventually the soldiers demanded sound money as payment. Ruling by force is not a position of strength. Any parent knows this.

Successful leadership means instilling trust. People trust certainty. Money certainty means creating a standard and sticking to it.

Currency Debasement Is the Same Throughout History

As the Western Roman Empire cascaded into instability, the Eastern Empire rosc. From the 4th century forward, the Byzantine Empire thrived.

Its capital, Constantinople, had the power to create coinage just like Rome. At first, its coins held steady value. With a high gold content, citizens trusted the money with their savings. After all, in the early days it watched money troubles unseat Rome from its dominant position.

Eventually everyone forgets about the last debasement. Enough time passes, people die, and nobody remembers the problems of the past.

In the 11th century a moneychanger named Michael IV the Paphlagonian took control of the empire. Within 40 years the empire's coinage fell from 87.5% pure gold to less than 30%. In the end, a small child could bend Byzantine coins made of flimsy, cheap metal.

With its money in crisis a new emperor took over at the end of the century. He returned the coinage to 90% pure gold.

This process repeats through all of history.

Governments Can't Resist

The trick is knowing when the debasement speeds up to an extreme.

The first debasements can be wildly profitable for people in the know. Take the Romans for example. Cutting 5% of silver content from the denarius gave the wealthy a boost at first. Once people caught on, trust faded. At the end, only force compels someone to take the worthless coins.

This can and will happen to the U.S. dollar. It won't be the first time.

Chapter 4 – 1933 Gold Confiscation

My grandfather G.S. Tucker Jr. taught me about the stock market. The night before he died in 2013, he read a printed copy of my first financial newsletter. It went out to roughly 300,000 paid subscribers. While I'll never know for sure, I sensed reading that letter he knew the student had become the teacher.

We were very close. We talked about everything, even taboo subjects the rest of my family wouldn't dare touch.

Born in 1919, he lived through an unprecedented period of economic growth. One point of contention in our close relationship was gold. He just didn't see the point. However, he often told me a story from his youth that made a strong argument for it.

In 1933 his mother gathered her four children together. At 14, he was the youngest. She had a cigar box filled with gold coins. They were mostly U.S. and European coins from the 18th and 19th centuries.

He described the coins in the box, including the one he kept. We estimated the box today would be worth around $1 million. Maybe more depending on the rarity and condition of the coins. (That was also over a decade ago when gold traded for half its current price. There's a strong argument for holding on to rare gold coins, which we'll discuss later.)

She told the kids they could each pick one coin to keep as a souvenir. At that time, the official price of gold was $20.67/oz.

She called it a souvenir because on March 9, 1933 President Franklin D. Roosevelt issued an executive order declaring gold effectively illegal. Going forward, citizens could keep no more than five ounces. All other gold had to be exchanged at any bank for $20.67/oz before May 1, 1933. Anyone holding gold after that time faced a fine of $10,000 and 10 years in prison.

POSTMASTER: PLEASE POST IN A CONSPICUOUS PLACE.—JAMES A. FARLEY, Postmaster General

UNDER EXECUTIVE ORDER OF THE PRESIDENT

issued April 5, 1933

all persons are required to deliver

ON OR BEFORE MAY 1, 1933

all GOLD COIN, GOLD BULLION, AND GOLD CERTIFICATES now owned by them to a Federal Reserve Bank, branch or agency, or to any member bank of the Federal Reserve System.

Executive Order

FORBIDDING THE HOARDING OF GOLD COIN, GOLD BULLION AND GOLD CERTIFICATES.

By virtue of the authority vested in me by Section 5(b) of the Act of October 6, 1917, as amended by Section 2 of the Act of March 9, 1933, entitled "An Act to provide relief in the existing national emergency in banking, and for other purposes", in which amendatory Act Congress declared that a serious emergency exists, I, Franklin D. Roosevelt, President of the United States of America, do declare that said national emergency still continues to exist and pursuant to said section do hereby prohibit the hoarding of gold coin, gold bullion, and gold certificates within the continental United States by individuals, partnerships, associations and corporations and hereby prescribe the following regulations for carrying out the purposes of this order:

Section 1. For the purposes of this regulation, the term "hoarding" means the withdrawal and withholding of gold coin, gold bullion or gold certificates from the recognized and customary channels of trade. The term "person" means any individual, partnership, association or corporation.

Section 2. All persons are hereby required to deliver on or before May 1, 1933, to a Federal reserve bank or a branch or agency thereof or to any member bank of the Federal Reserve System all gold coin, gold bullion and gold certificates now owned by them or coming into their ownership on or before April 28, 1933, except the following:

(a) Such amount of gold as may be required for legitimate and customary use in industry, profession or art within a reasonable time, including gold prior to refining and stocks of gold in reasonable amounts for the usual trade requirements of owners mining and refining such gold.

(b) Gold coin and gold certificates in an amount not exceeding in the aggregate $100.00 belonging to any one person; and gold coins having a recognized special value to collectors of rare and unusual coins.

(c) Gold coin and bullion earmarked or held in trust for a recognized foreign government or foreign central bank or the Bank for International Settlements.

(d) Gold coin and bullion licensed for other proper transactions (not involving hoarding) including gold coin and bullion imported for reexport or held pending action on applications for export licenses.

Section 3. Until otherwise ordered any person becoming the owner of any gold coin, gold bullion, or gold certificates after April 28, 1933, shall, within three days after receipt thereof, deliver the same in the manner prescribed in Section 2; unless such gold coin, gold bullion or gold certificates are held for any of the purposes specified in paragraphs (a), (b) or (c) of Section 2; or unless such gold coin or gold bullion is held for purposes specified in paragraph (d) of Section 2 and the person holding it is, with respect to such gold coin or bullion, a licensee or applicant for license pending action thereon.

Section 4. Upon receipt of gold coin, gold bullion or gold certificates delivered to it in accordance with Sections 2 or 3, the Federal reserve bank or member bank will pay therefor an equivalent amount of any other form of coin or currency coined or issued under the laws of the United States.

Section 5. Member banks shall deliver all gold coin, gold bullion and gold certificates owned or received by them (other than as exempted under the provisions of Section 2) to the Federal reserve banks of their respective districts and receive credit or payment therefor.

Section 6. The Secretary of the Treasury, out of the sum made available to the President by Section 501 of the Act of March 9, 1933, will in all proper cases pay the reasonable costs of transportation of gold coin, gold bullion or gold certificates delivered to a member bank or Federal reserve bank in accordance with Sections 2, 3, or 5 hereof, including the cost of insurance, protection, and such other incidental costs as may be necessary, upon production of satisfactory evidence of such costs. Voucher forms for this purpose may be procured from Federal reserve banks.

Section 7. In cases where the delivery of gold coin, gold bullion or gold certificates by the owners thereof within the time set forth above will involve extraordinary hardship or difficulty, the Secretary of the Treasury may, in his discretion, extend the time within which such delivery must be made. Applications for such extensions must be made in writing under oath, addressed to the Secretary of the Treasury and filed with a Federal reserve bank. Each application must state the date to which the extension is desired, the amount and location of the gold coin, gold bullion and gold certificates in respect of which such application is made and the facts showing extension to be necessary to avoid extraordinary hardship or difficulty.

Section 8. The Secretary of the Treasury is hereby authorized and empowered to issue such further regulations as he may deem necessary to carry out the purposes of this order and to issue licenses thereunder, through such officers or agencies as he may designate, including licenses permitting the Federal reserve banks and member banks of the Federal Reserve System, in return for an equivalent amount of other coin, currency or credit, to deliver, earmark or hold in trust gold coin and bullion to or for persons showing the need for the same for any of the purposes specified in paragraphs (a), (c) and (d) of Section 2 of these regulations.

Section 9. Whoever willfully violates any provision of this Executive Order or of these regulations or of any rule, regulation or license issued thereunder may be fined not more than $10,000, or, if a natural person, may be imprisoned for not more than ten years, or both; and any officer, director, or agent of any corporation who knowingly participates in any such violation may be punished by a like fine, imprisonment, or both.

This order and these regulations may be modified or revoked at any time.

THE WHITE HOUSE
April 5, 1933.

FRANKLIN D ROOSEVELT

For Further Information Consult Your Local Bank

GOLD CERTIFICATES may be identified by the words "GOLD CERTIFICATE" appearing thereon. The serial number and the Treasury seal on the face of a GOLD CERTIFICATE are printed in YELLOW. Be careful not to confuse GOLD CERTIFICATES with other issues which are redeemable in gold but which are not GOLD CERTIFICATES. Federal Reserve Notes and United States Notes are "redeemable in gold" but are not "GOLD CERTIFICATES" and are not required to be surrendered

Special attention is directed to the exceptions allowed under Section 2 of the Executive Order

CRIMINAL PENALTIES FOR VIOLATION OF EXECUTIVE ORDER $10,000 fine or 10 years imprisonment, or both, as provided in Section 9 of the order

W. H. Woodin
Secretary of the Treasury.

U.S. Government Printing Office: 1933 2-16064

I asked my grandfather why his mother complied with this.

He said his mother felt President Roosevelt asked for the gold because the country needed it. In her mind, defying the order would be an act of treason. She wasn't totally off base. Executive Order 6102 took its legal basis from the 1917 Trading with the Enemy Act.

After issuing the order in March 1933 Roosevelt had the country's major newspapers support the action with daily articles about gold hoarders. These "speculators" put the nation in danger according to the media drumbeat. It's easy to see why my great grandmother took the order seriously.

How to Debase the U.S. Dollar

Shortly after confiscating gold from his citizens at a price of $20.67/oz, Roosevelt revalued gold to $35/oz.

To be clear, this means the official value of gold rose 69% by decree. It took that many more dollars to equal the same gold ounce. The value of the gold stayed the same, it's the dollar that lost value.

Keep in mind, gold did not trade on the domestic market in the U.S. There was no quote for the gold price as there is today. It had a fixed price of $20.67/oz before the 1933 confiscation order. The price was $35/oz after the order. After May 1, 1933 it was illegal to own gold outside of a few souvenir ounces.

What citizens didn't realize at the time was Roosevelt needed their gold in order to devalue the dollar. This means debase the dollar. As in Roman times, debasement was the only way out for governments in money trouble.

1933 was the official tail end of the Great Depression. The stock market crash of 1929 merely kicked off the economic decline. What people didn't realize was the 1929 crash was a warning to get out and stay out of the market. Over the next few years people lost their life savings jumping back into the market only to see it fall more.

During the Depression years gold held a fixed value of $20.67. Businesses failed in droves. the U.S. unemployment rate hit 22%. It stayed high. There was no work. With the value of all other assets falling precipitously, gold sat flat.

That means the value of $1,000 worth of stock (roughly $20,000 in today's dollars) fell in some cases to almost nothing, while the value of $1,000 worth of gold remained $1,000.

That put the Federal Reserve in a tough spot. The Fed was a fairly new creation at the time. It formed in 1913, just 20 years prior. That move ceded control of U.S. money to a consortium of private bankers.

It was a tough sell to the people in 1913. Part of the compromise was in limiting the Fed's ability to create money. Initially, dollars created were 40% backed by gold.

The deflationary years of the Great Depression pressured the newly created Fed's dollar system. Major banks sometimes had to sell gold as there was nothing else left holding value.

In a deflation, prices fall lower and lower. There is no demand for business services, and prices keep falling until buyers emerge. In the worst imaginable scenario, there are no buyers at any price.

With the country mired in a deflationary spiral FDR needed a weaker dollar. This might sound familiar as today politicians all clamor for a weak currency.

Think back to the Romans. Imagine borrowing 1,000 denarii made of silver. When the loan comes due you pay it back with worthless coins made of bronze. For the borrower, this is a major win. For the lender, it's a big loss.

Buying all the privately-owned gold in the U.S. for $20.67/oz and immediately revaluing it to $35/oz meant FDR effectively devalued the dollar by 69%. He did that almost overnight. All it took was one executive order, a few pointed editorials from helpful members of the media, and the power to compel his citizens.

At some point today's U.S. government will face a similar dilemma. When that day comes, it's too late to prepare.

Chapter 5 – 1944 The Golden Rule

The person with the gold makes the rules. The same goes for countries.

In 1944 leaders from 44 allied nations gathered at a posh hotel in the mountains of New Hampshire to plot a new world monetary system. The initial meeting happened just around the time U.S. troops landed at Normandy.

The U.S. entered World War II years into the fighting. Nations on both sides of the conflict drained their treasuries, borrowed from allies and sacrificed everything before U.S. troops formally engaged. This gave the U.S. a financial upper hand in negotiating the post-war financial system.

At the time, the U.S. had control of roughly 40% of total estimated world gold supplies. That was largely thanks to successfully confiscating gold from its citizens the decade prior.

The New Hampshire meeting goes by the name Bretton Woods, the name of the hotel where delegates gathered.

The new monetary order would effectively rid the world of any gold standard. "Gold standard" is frequently thrown around in conversation and it's almost always incorrectly used.

A gold standard means currency issuance ties directly to a country's gold reserves. The U.S. did at one time have such a standard. It essentially cut that standard in 1933 when FDR debased the U.S. currency by confiscating gold and forbidding private ownership in the U.S. The 1944 meeting set up the gold-to-dollar exchange which went into place in 1945 and held until 1971.

For starters, the 1944 meeting established the International Monetary Fund (IMF) and the World Bank. Both entities would facilitate post-war rebuilding. The U.S. would have de facto control since it held the world's largest gold reserves. That gold played an important role in the plan.

At the time, war-ravaged nations of the world all had their own currency. Drachma, lira, dinar, franc, pound, Reichsmark... were all effectively worthless. This was long before the days of the Euro. Keeping track of hundreds of weak exchange rates would be impossible as the world rebuilt.

The U.S. would use its gold hoard to create an exchange standard. At any time, foreign banks, foreign governments, and certain foreign entities could present the U.S. Federal Reserve with $35 dollars and receive one ounce of U.S. gold in return. This "exchange standard" would stabilize the currencies of the world when it came to post-war trade.

Say post-war Greece and Italy needed to negotiate a trade agreement. The Greek drachma would have a quoted exchange value to dollars. The Italian lira would have one too. With the dollar as a base for establishing a trusted value for all currencies, the two countries could deal. They didn't have to fear sudden devaluation altering the terms.

The U.S. dollar would be the denominator of world trade. With a fixed exchange to gold at $35/oz all other countries could rebuild, devalue and organize their economies with certainty.

The only catch was the U.S. would need to behave itself financially or lose its gold.

Spending Other People's Money Is Easy

The 1944 Bretton Woods meeting cemented the U.S. as the world's financial anchor. This was a power almost unimaginable in history, one the U.S. managed to hold on to it until 1971.

Recall the terms, a foreign financial entity could exchange $35 of U.S. currency for an ounce of gold. When the agreement went into place, dollars had gold-like power. The U.S. held a controlling share of the world's physical gold.

Meanwhile, U.S. citizens faced felony charges for owning gold. That meant the U.S. government had the ability to effectively control world trade without its citizens supervising.

When gold trades in a free market, buyers and sellers set the price. This is called "price discovery" as the free market finds a fair price. With gold pegged at a fixed price there was no market. This amounted to unchecked power for the U.S.

Slowly, the U.S. overspent. Governments can't help themselves. First millions, then billions of dollars crept overseas.

The extra spending started small. For instance, the Employment Act of 1946 expanded the Fed's powers to include monitoring employment and other economic activity. While the U.S. touted free markets around the world, politicians thought it would be nice to have the central bank softening the blow if the economy ran into any trouble. Just like today, leaders promised any financial accommodation would be temporary.

Next came the Korean War, which was largely under control compared to the cost of modern military action. The real trouble started after Eisenhower left office.

Kennedy stepped in as the memory of the troublesome 1930s began to fade. A new generation only knew stories of the Great Depression. A compassionate U.S. government started programs to feed and care for giant swaths of its underclass.

After Kennedy's death Johnson carried on with Great Society spending programs. The country fell deeper and deeper into the Vietnam conflict. Domestic budget deficits at home and ballooning spending in Southeast Asia flooded the world with dollars.

Wisely, foreign institutions gathered up those dollars returning them to the government's gold exchange window. They'd hand over $35 for an ounce of U.S. gold. Slowly the country's massive gold hoard dwindled.

Silver supplies also dwindled. As excess dollars escaped into the world foreigners exchanged them for U.S. silver fixed at $1.29/oz.

Until 1964 the U.S. used silver to make its coins. Just like the Romans, they had to stop.

Debase the Coins

U.S. dollar coins, half-dollars, quarters, and dimes contained 90% silver. Nickels of some years had 35%. Until 1964.

With its money still tied to precious metals, foreign entities preyed on U.S. deficit spending. As it spent more and more those dollars came back in exchange for gold and silver. The pace picked up over time.

By 1964 the value of silver in U.S. coins was greater than the coin's face value. That meant the change in people's pockets was worth more as melted silver than as payment for groceries.

Specifically, four quarters had a value of $1.00 in the checkout line. Melting those quarters down and selling the silver content yielded more than $1.00. The consequences of borrowing beyond its means came home to roost for the U.S., but its citizens were the last to know. Foreign entities had a better view of the dollar's declining value. They quickly took advantage of the situation.

The Coinage Act of 1965 put an end to this. It removed silver from dimes and quarters. It reduced silver content in half-dollars to 40%. Five years later it took that to 0%.

Most Americans did not know about the dwindling silver supplies. They also didn't care. Through those years thousands of soldiers died in a barbaric proxy war half-way around the world.

Emotions tied to Vietnam still run high. I know a local coin dealer who served and it's a subject that can't come up. It's too bad we can't talk about Vietnam. From a monetary perspective, it's critically important.

Vietnam was a trap. The U.S. stepped in the trap with one foot. Instead of cutting off the foot, the U.S. forced in the other foot. Then its hands, finally its head.

To be clear, Vietnam was the end of U.S. monetary supremacy, not the cause.

In 1944 the U.S. anchored the world monetary system. Discipline and absolute power don't mix well. At first, abuses are small. Then they grow. The competing personalities involved have their own incentives. Excess spending becomes a one-way street.

Fully entrenched in Vietnam, 25 years of foreign efforts to lure excess dollars out of the U.S. reached an extreme. Under the Bretton Woods gold exchange agreement, the U.S. saw 65% of its gold fly away and never return. As the pace of gold flows ramped up, there was no choice but to end the gold-dollar exchange.

Chapter 6 – 1971 Nixon's Sunday Night Devaluation

On Sunday evening August 15, 1971 President Richard Nixon officially devalued the savings and earning power of every American. It took only 18 minutes. Almost no one noticed.

Of course, they heard the speech. It aired live on every major radio and television station in the country. The problem is, Nixon did a masterful job disguising the well-orchestrated devaluation from the average American.

He ended the ability for foreign banks to convert dollars to gold. Until that moment foreign banks could exchange $35 for an ounce of U.S. gold. That meant the U.S. dollar maintained a fixed value tied to the gold price. With this removed, the world would now value the dollar based on its true worth, not its convertibility into gold. Nixon knew that meant a sudden plunge in value for the dollar.

In fairness, he had no choice. The damage was done.

To recap, with the Bretton Woods agreement 26 years prior, allied nations of the world agreed to a new monetary order. The post-war world needed a stable currency system to facilitate rebuilding.

The U.S. started out with a position rarely seen in world history. The post-war dollar was as good as gold.

The U.S. had 60% of the world's official gold reserves at the time. That's over 22,000 metric tons. It agreed to exchange $35 for one ounce of that gold at any time. Only foreign banks could access this mechanism called the exchange window.

Spending programs of the 1950s and 1960s pushed the federal budget into deficit. The deficit grew slowly at first, then quickly. The Vietnam War pushed deficit spending into overdrive.

Deficit spending means more dollars flowing out of the treasury than tax revenue coming in to support them. Foreign governments and central banks eagerly exchanged the dollars held on their books for gold at the U.S. exchange window.

When Nixon hit the airwaves that night the massive U.S. gold hoard was 63% smaller than when the gold-to-dollar exchange agreement went in place 26 years prior.

Words Matter

U.S. leaders knew the dollar was in trouble. Once convertibility to gold ended it would find its true value. That was far lower than 1/35th of an ounce of gold.

Nixon had to sell this to the people. He called his speech, "The challenge of peace."

He talked about soldiers unable to find work after returning from victory in Vietnam. Bringing the war up was a distraction. In reality, it raged on for at least four more years after the speech.

Next, he talked about inflation. The Consumer Price Index (CPI) rose 6% per year for five years leading up to his speech. He promised to break that trend and help average people get by.

He positioned himself as a hero. All good fiction needs a hero and a villain. The villain, as he told it, was a cabal of "international money speculators." He made them sound terrible. They raised prices at the grocery store. They kept veterans from finding work. Neither was true.

The truth was, the U.S. had an incredible power as the world's bedrock currency following the Bretton Woods agreement. Its gold hoard underpinned this power. It abused the position by running persistent budget deficits. Foreign banks wisely swapped dollars for gold.

Just as FDR disguised the 1933 devaluation by blaming it on treasonous hoarders, Nixon blamed external factors. He pretended to stand up for hard-working Americans.

In both cases, 1933 and 1971, U.S. leaders abused the nation's money for years before sticking the bill on its citizens. The actual devaluations were inevitable.

What Devaluation Looks Like

Over halfway through the speech Nixon said, "I want to lay to rest this bugaboo called devaluation." He knew what was about to happen to the average American's wealth.

Here's what it looked like over time. The following chart tracks the value of the U.S. dollar against currencies of other nations. The arrow in the chart marks the time leading up to Nixon's speech.

As the chart shows, the value of the dollar fell for months leading up to Nixon's official announcement.

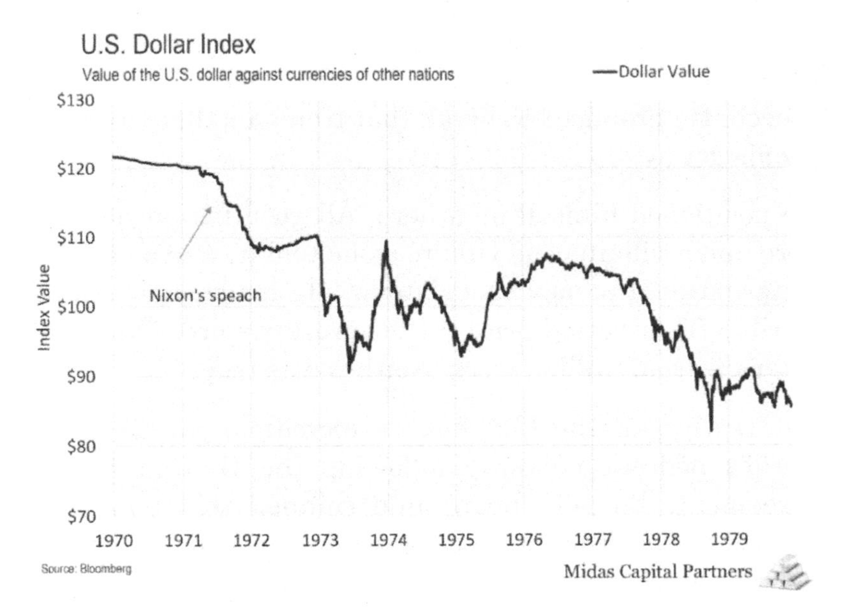

Recall that Nixon said the evil speculators relentlessly attacked the dollar in the weeks prior to his speech. We can only assume that U.S. deficit spending hit a level so extreme foreign governments lost confidence. There was a rush to grab U.S. gold.

The door to the now much-smaller U.S. gold vault closed after the speech.

With the dollar peg to gold officially removed, the value of the U.S. currency fell precipitously against those of other nations.

Lucky for Nixon People Don't Understand Currencies

In March 2016 I took my sister on a ski trip to Switzerland. She's easy to travel with and wanted to see what it was like to ski on real mountains.

We started out at St. Moritz. At lunch on day two I said, "This afternoon we're both going to buy a Rolex."

My sister wasn't interested. She didn't care for watches. She's also, wisely, quite frugal. I took her to the store anyway.

On the way I explained the Swiss franc was near parity with the U.S. dollar. The summer prior it was 10% higher.

When I visited in 2011, it was 25% higher. She still didn't quite understand my enthusiasm. Instead of teaching her about the value of currencies, I'd let her learn.

She picked out a nice watch. Priced in Swiss francs, we calculated the conversion rate to dollars. She'd pay about $4,000 for the watch.

I told her to go outside and call the Rolex dealer at the local mall in Florida. Tell them she's looking for a price quote on that exact model. Don't bother mentioning she's in Switzerland.

She came back in the store told me, "You won't believe it, this watch is $5,000 in Florida!"

Rolex prices watches using the Manufacturer's Suggested Retail Price (MSRP). That means it sets the watch price for a period of time and doesn't make a lot of changes. My hunch was, with the value of the franc down, our dollars would buy more watch than even one year prior.

That turned out to be true. I bought a watch too. My price was 19% less than I'd pay back in Florida.

My point here is, most people don't understand how the value of currencies fluctuate. If you're only spending dollars, you never leave the U.S. and don't plan to consume any products from abroad, you'll never notice a currency devaluation.

"If You're One of Those People"

In his devaluation speech, Nixon made reference to, "those people." He chided those who might want to buy a foreign car or take a trip to London.

This is a classic tactic in class warfare. It's an attempt to pit the masses against a wealthy minority. He's insinuating the housewife battling grocery inflation has it tough because the corporate executive wants to take his wife to Wimbledon. In reality, the two have nothing to do with one another.

In fact, the corporate executive could have, and should have, exchanged as many dollars as possible while overseas during the years leading up to Nixon's 1971 devaluation. To any thinking person, the devaluation was obvious. Fortunately for Nixon and other politicians, the ranks of the thinking are thin.

To shield the public from watching their dollar tumble in value, he asked Congress to impose several distractions.

First, he asked for a 10% tariff on all imported foreign goods. He said this would protect the American worker from international evils. The truth is, it masked part of the dollar's 25% tumble between 1970 and 1973. Tariffs and taxes on imported goods are a political tool to obscure their changing value.

Second, he proposed a freeze on all price increases for 90 days. Nothing obscures the free market price like making something illegal. This bought him a few months of political reprieve. Businesses could cushion the blow as the dollar tumbled.

Remember, raw materials like copper, oil, gold, and anything used by every country trade on a world market.

Regardless of currency, buyers must pay the going rate to get these materials. While Nixon stopped the price of butter from rising, he couldn't hold back the built-up inflationary tidal wave. Years in the making, it was about to destroy the U.S. turning the 1970s into a tumultuous decade for unprepared dollar holders.

Chapter 7 – 1970-1979 Gold Gains 1,365%

The U.S. dollar lost its tether to gold in August 1971. Nixon scrambled to enact laws preventing Americans from seeing the dollar's true value. Meanwhile, it was still a felony for U.S. citizens to own gold.

Gold has a special value. It's immune from the devaluation tactics that plague government-issued money.

Gold can sit at the bottom of the ocean for millennia. Pull it up, dry it off, and every molecule of gold is still intact.

Physically speaking, gold has integrity. It keeps its shape during a 1,000-degree house fire. To melt it you'll need 1,948-degrees of heat. While its shape will change, its weight does not. That means its real value stays intact.

Theft and government seizure are the only true perils for gold. FDR's gold seizure in 1933 made possessing it a felony. As the dollar tumbled in value during the early 1970s, informed Americans started asking questions.

A New Orleans-based gold advocate named Jim Blanchard organized a gold legalization movement. He hired a plane to fly a giant banner over Richard Nixon's January 1973 inauguration.

Source: goldnewsletter.com

What Blanchard and others realized was keeping gold illegal kept Americans in the dark about the real value of their dollars. Again, if you don't travel, don't buy international goods, and don't deal in international commodities, you probably won't notice a currency devaluation until it's too late. In the 1970's, that's just what the U.S. government wanted.

The Scramble to Find Cheaper Imports

Six months after Nixon cut the dollar's peg to gold, he flew to China. This was a historic visit. He made sure to get the most out of photos and media coverage of his diplomatic mission.

On the surface, Nixon would improve world relations. He reestablished ties with China after decades of tension.

The truth about this trip was Nixon knew opening China was the only way to soften the blow of dollar weakness. When I say "Nixon," I don't mean he himself thought this up.

U.S. presidents don't have the power most people assume they do. There are competing forces pushing and clawing for advantage in the U.S. The same goes for all nations. This is the nature of things. It's no different from 10 puppies fighting over 8 teats.

The U.S. standard of living was in trouble in the 70s. Three decades of overspending caught up to the average American in an instant. To mask the problem, it needed cheaper access to consumer goods and energy.

China could solve the first problem. Mao Zedong had the giant nation fully under his thumb. U.S. media outlets largely ignored his murderous grip on power. Mao murdered by the thousands.

The State Department issued a friendly estimate of Mao's killing spree at 800,000 victims. He himself guessed he killed 700,000 of his own citizens. Outside accounts were closer to 1.5 million people.

Mass murder, genocide and human rights only matter to the U.S. when there are political benefits on the line. They go right under the rug when it needs something else. In this case, it needed a giant factory to produce cheap goods in exchange for weak U.S. dollars in the years to come. China was in.

Gold Becomes Legal

Nixon left office in August 1974. It was almost three years from the day he cut the dollar's link to gold.

President Gerald Ford took office on August 9, 1974. Just six days later he signed Public Law 93-373 making gold ownership legal for American citizens. The law went into effect on December 31 of that year.

As the next chart shows, after 41 years of carrying a felony charge for ownership, U.S. citizens could once again own gold.

Law-abiding Americans missed out on the first few years of the gold rally. When Nixon removed the peg in 1971 gold was $35/oz. The day it became legal to own it sold for $183.85/oz.

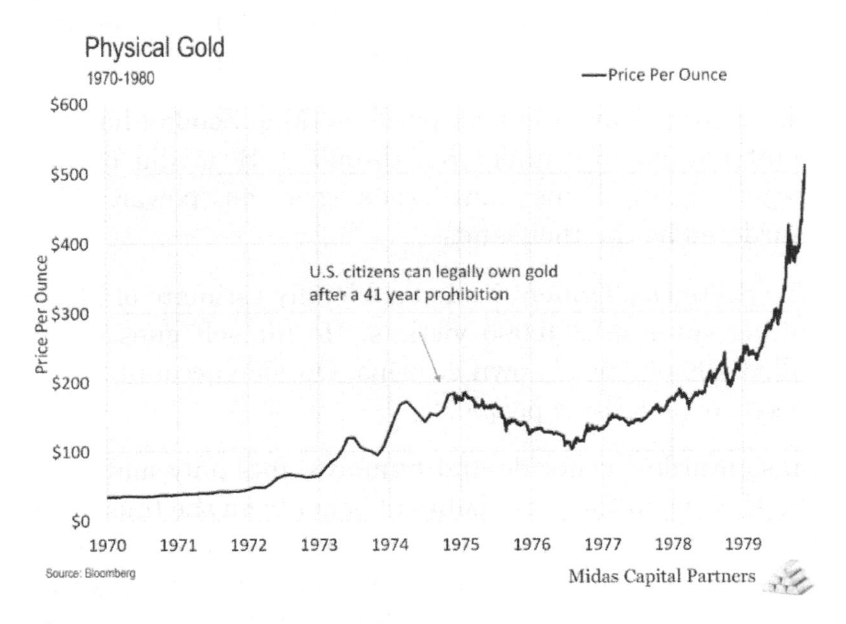

The rumor of legalization sent gold prices soaring in advance of the new law. That's common in markets. The rumor of a policy change can send prices soaring higher than the news of the change itself.

Illegal for 41 years, most people in the U.S. didn't understand gold. It seemed like something a country would own. The idea that anyone would need it to protect their wealth didn't register. By the end of the decade, everyone would understand the value of gold.

After initially shooting up 400% between 1971 and legalization in 1974, gold settled down. It drifted slowly lower for about 18 months. This was the time to buy. In the late years of the 1970s it would go on an epic run topping out at $850/oz in January 1980. Bottom to top that marked a 23-fold increase from its formerly fixed value of $35/oz.

Gold mining stocks ran even more. For decades, companies producing gold sold it into a fixed market. Towards the end of the gold dollar exchange gold mining was a tough business. Costs rose faster than revenue due to the fixed price.

That changed as the gold price took off. Long-life mines sold output for a multiple of initial projections. Imagine what would happen to your business if you raised prices by more than 20 times and the only consequence was customer interest tripled. That's what happened to gold miners in the late 1970s.

We're about to experience something similar today.

There's the Bottom, Then the Test

George Soros has a famous quote about markets that says, "There's the bottom, then the test."

I flew to the Bahamas in January 2020 to meet with a famous investor. He's an unrivaled thinker, market strategist, and gentleman. We dined at his palatial home where we talked about gold.

We both felt that gold looked set to explode in price. Our estimate turned out to be right. That said, there's a long way to go.

My host reminded me of what George Soros said about markets, and how it related to certain times in the gold market. The bottom is hard to pick, only a daredevil tries to nail it exactly. Then there's the first run. In the previous chart, that was 1971-1974 in the run up to legalization.

Then, there's the test. People who got the gold story right in 1974 faced this test. They got the big picture right buying gold. By the end of the decade they'd see much higher prices. But first, they'd endure 18 months where the price drifted lower before taking off.

The test is always painful. Many people can't handle it. They sell, walk away, and try to forget about the idea entirely. The more intense the test, the more spectacular the rally. The reward comes to those who get it right and have patience.

After becoming legal in 1974, gold fell 44% through August 1976. Owners who held the newly legal metal questioned their thinking. Those who survived the test went on to see a 721% rally in the three and a half years that followed.

We're in a similar period today. Gold hit an all-time high of $1,900/oz in September 2011. It spent the next four years slowly falling. In December 2015 it hit a low of $1,050/oz. That was a long and painful test.

In the three years that followed the December 2015 bottom it ran quietly without much notice. In December 2018, major gold dealer Kitco Metals interviewed me on the subject. Gold sat right around $1,250/oz at the time.

I told the host gold looked set to breach $1,500/oz the following year. It hit that mark less than eight months later. That was a more than 20% advance that was barely noticed in the mainstream financial news.

I went back on the same Kitco program calling for $1,900/oz in 2020. Three months in gold topped $1,700/oz again with little mainstream attention.

What I hope you see by the end of this book is it's merely the warm-up phase of the current gold bull market. It has a lot farther to run.

Just as in 1971, a devaluation is on the horizon. Investors who see that now, in advance of the official news, stand the chance to earn substantial profits. More importantly, they'll preserve their hard-earned wealth.

Chapter 8 – 1985 The Plaza Hotel Fix

In late 2016 I flew to North Carolina to meet with a former top executive of BB&T bank (now Truist Financial). He teaches a class at a local business school.

He climbed the ranks at BB&T when its headquarters was in Wilson, NC. That's where I grew up. In fact, I carpooled to grade school with his kids.

My grandfather sat on the bank's board for years. He thought highly of the group chosen to run things when he and his peers retired. They went on to multiply the size of what had been a small North Carolina bank.

Wilson is a small tobacco town about one hour east of Raleigh, the state capital. The bank left in the mid-90s. The tobacco market did too. Today it's essentially impoverished.

The group that transformed the bank into a major institution wasn't what you'd expect. Knowing them well, it's fair to say they were more libertarian-minded than their peers.

During our meeting, I brought up gold. It was $1,250/oz at the time. We were about to form Metalla Royalty & Streaming (MTA) in what I felt was a once in a lifetime chance to acquire royalties on future gold production. I wanted to test my thinking on someone with a storied banking career.

I laid out what I saw coming for the financial system, the incentives in place and how I expected they'd shape the future. To me, the course looked inevitable. If that's how it played out, gold would be an essential investment.

To assure me I wasn't far off, he told me a story about dealing with banking regulators. They're testy, by-the-book types. They'd visit the bank routinely to look over its financials.

During one visit he asked the regulator, "Why doesn't the government fix the price of oranges." The regulator snapped back instantly telling him we'd never allow that in the U.S. because this is a free market. That's why the country is so powerful, so filled with opportunity. My host's reply, "Hmm, well, why do you (the Fed) fix the price of money?"

He only did this once. While I thought this was a brilliant question, he said it didn't go over well. The sentries who polish the façade of the U.S. financial system don't take kindly to intellectual sparring.

Obviously, fixing the price of oranges would reward bad producers and punish premium producers.

Say the fixed price was $1/lb. Growers of sub-par orange crops that normally sold for $0.75/lb get a profit boost. Meanwhile, growers of premium oranges that once sold for $1.25/lb would take a crippling loss.

The incentives in this case reward growers who produce the cheapest crop possible. Over time you'd see a black market for quality oranges emerge. That underground black market would be a true free market, with prices set by buyers willing to pay up for quality.

The question my friend asked his regulators that day has important philosophical meaning. Understanding what this means will help you see what's ahead for today's monetary system which is no longer a free market.

Price fixing is exactly what governments do with their money. The U.S. is the worst offender.

How to Spot What's Ahead

When Nixon ended dollar convertibility to gold in August 1971, the damage was already done. Waiting any longer would have emptied the U.S. gold vault entirely.

People paying attention in the years leading up to his speech expected this, or something similar. It's difficult to predict exactly when this type of event will happen in the markets, but how it will happen is a bit easier.

After Nixon's 1971 speech the U.S. dollar lost 23% of its value against rival currencies. That planted the seeds of radical price inflation, energy market instability and general economic malaise that turned up later in the decade.

That's the trick to getting in front of a major market move. If you can see the seeds planted, you'll know in advance where to look for the mature plants.

By the end of the 1970s, the average American stood by bamboozled at the sight of gas lines, shortages and sky-high interest rates. Gold, the only protection against circumstances like these, topped out at $850/oz the day after Reagan's 1980 inauguration. By then it was too late to seek shelter from the economic storm.

People tend to base their thoughts about the economic future on what just happened. They're somehow unable to see the early stages of change and consider what's ahead.

In 1971 they didn't see the tumultuous decade ahead. In 1980 they felt the turmoil would never end. Both times they got it wrong.

I know this firsthand. I have two very smart friends in their early 70s. Both are renowned investors. They don't know each other personally, but both were up and coming financial analysts during the late 1970s.

The first, Doug Casey, wrote a book called *Crisis Investing*. The theme was the radical inflation and economic turmoil of the 1970s was just the tip of the iceberg. Crisis Investing was a *New York Times* bestseller. Doug appeared on many major television and radio programs. While the book is incredibly insightful, his general premise did not play out in the following years.

At almost the exact same time, unbeknownst to Casey, Kiril Sokoloff and A. Gary Shilling wrote a book titled *Inflation is Ending: Are you Ready?* This book proposed the turmoil of the 1970s was effectively over. Stocks would surge after a decade of literally going nowhere. Interest rates would fall from 15% to far lower levels. While deadly accurate, this book sold far fewer copies. The public preferred a book predicting more of the same ahead.

Part of what Sokoloff and Shilling realized was that structural changes like the 1979 appointment of Paul Volker to Fed Chairman were major turning points. For instance, Volker took steps to break the back of inflation. This meant gold, commodities and hard asset investing had run its course. It was time to buy what nobody wanted, stocks, bonds, and assets that benefit from a stronger U.S. dollar.

The reforms of the late 1970s were lost on the average American. It was too late to profit once they finally noticed. They piled into gold, silver and anything that promised protection from a falling dollar and high inflation. Already visible on the horizon, they could not see a major change ahead.

Strong, but Not Too Strong

By 1981 things turned around for the beleaguered U.S. dollar.

High interest rates broke the back of inflation. Borrowing costs peaked and began to fall. By 1982 the bottom was in for stocks. Assets that suffered in the prior decade started moving higher.

Mid-way through the decade the dollar doubled in value from its late-70s low. People finally dumped inflation protection assets for big losses, jumping back into the dollar. They now wanted a piece of the booming economy of the 1980s.

Trips overseas, barely affordable for the wealthy five years prior, were cheap. The dollar had incredible value again against other currencies.

Then on September 22, 1985 representatives from the five largest economies at the time met at the Plaza Hotel on the southeast corner of Central Park in New York City. They agreed the dollar was too strong. They planned a coordinated effort to reduce its value. It was the second devaluation in 15 years.

As the next chart shows, by New Year's Eve 1987, the value of the dollar was back where it started the decade.

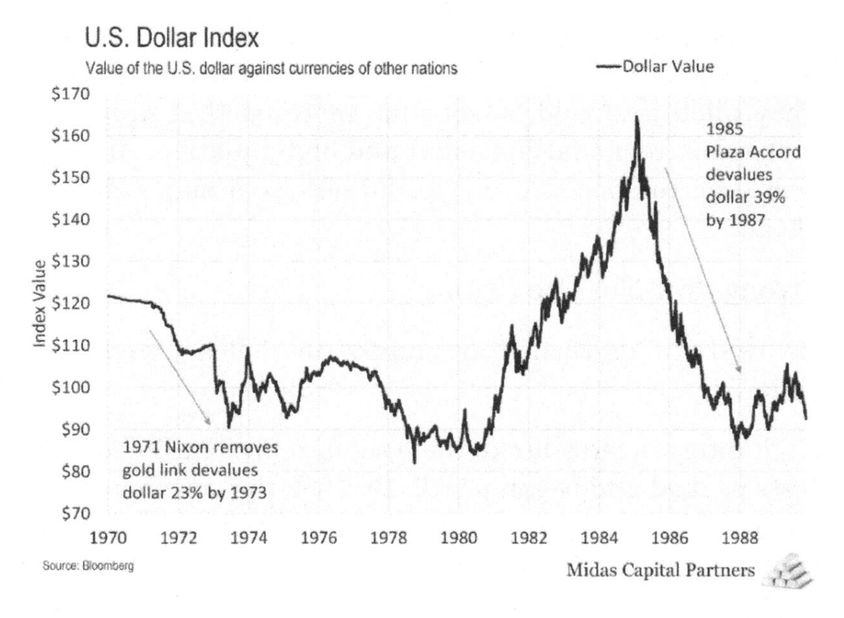

A strong dollar means its value towers over trading partners. Trips abroad, luxury imports, and a high standard of living for people with money are common with a strong dollar. However, the strong dollar makes U.S. exports expensive to overseas importers.

It's similar to my 2016 trip to Switzerland when the dollar gained on the Swiss franc. I took advantage by buying a Swiss watch priced in francs. The exchange worked to my advantage. My dollars had greater value.

At the same time, if a Swiss citizen flew to Aspen, Colorado, for a ski trip it would seem more expensive.

The truth today is, no country wants a strong currency. It's easy to see by scanning financial headlines. You'll notice governments accusing each other of "manipulating" currency values. None of them want to let the free market work. Anyone serious about preserving wealth must own assets immune to this government rollercoaster.

If the free market reigned, savers and investors would set the fair value of currencies. Undervalued countries would see a surge in international attention. For instance, if the Swiss franc fell too much, U.S. skiers would flock to the Alps.

Politicians won't allow the free market to work. They can't bear the social backlash that comes from a groaning public unaware of market trends.

The banking regulator said it best when asked why the government wouldn't fix the price of oranges. The free market naturally puts a premium on quality and a discount on junk.

However, he missed the point of the question. The government does tremendous damage by fixing the price of money and credit.

Chapter 9 – The Inevitable Devaluation

The evidence is clear. Governments spend money they don't have. When the bill comes due, they devalue their currency to pay it. It's a trend stretching back thousands of years.

For governments, the power to tax is paramount. Pay your taxes, or go to jail.

Taxes start small. In the U.S. there was no income tax until 1913. The law met heavy resistance. It took four years to ratify.

What starts small grows. Half-percent, then one, two, ten and finally, no amount is enough. The government always needs more to get the job done. It rarely spends that money wisely.

In 2019 the U.S. collected $3.46 trillion in taxes. That's over 16% of its GDP. It spent almost $1 trillion more than it collected in taxes. Borrowed money made up the difference.

Our concern, as wealth-builders bound to the government money system, is not bankruptcy. That's rare. A government like the U.S. can borrow to fund its ballooning budget for years to come. In fact, as long as it can compel the world to accept dollars, there's no limit to its spending addiction.

It's the value of the dollars we earn, save, and invest that deserves concern. The following chart shows the purchasing power of $1 dating back to 1900. As you can see, a $1-dollar bill today had over $30 worth of buying power in 1900.

Put simply, $1 went a long way in 1900. Saving up $1,000 back then was enough for a down payment on a nice house, a piece of land, or something significant. $1,000 in 1900 had the value of over $30,000 today.

However, if your ancestor stuck that hefty $1,000 savings in an envelope marked for you to open today it would barely cover one month of rent at a down-market apartment complex.

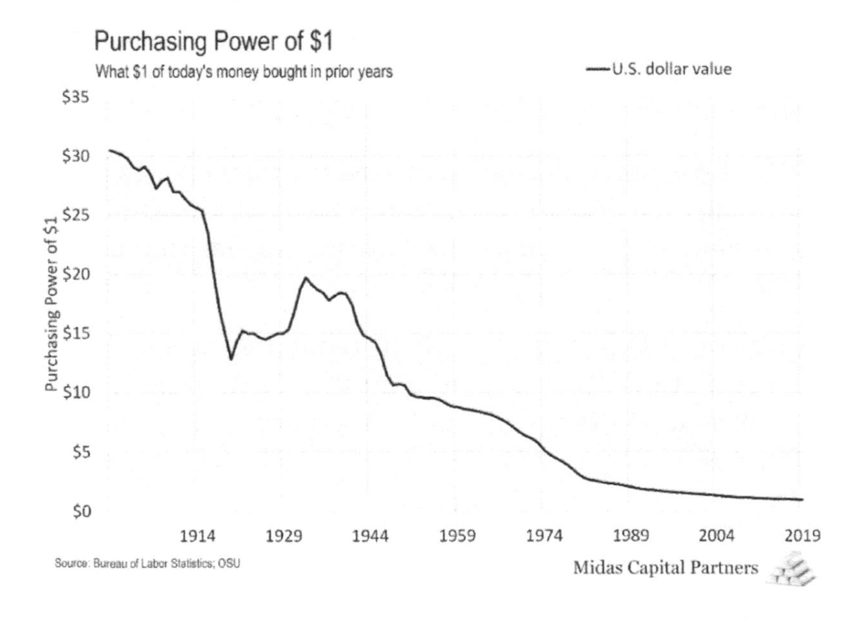

The value of government money doesn't look good over time. Hard work and savings erode through periodic devaluations.

There were key moments in the 20th century when dollar wealth sustained a serious blow. Holding gold during those periods meant preserving the purchasing power of wealth through those devaluations.

The next chart shows the value of one gold ounce going back to 1900. If your ancestor swapped the $1,000 of hard-earned savings for gold and put that in an envelope, you'd have 48 ounces of gold worth more than $80,000 today.

That means gold not only preserved wealth and purchasing power over the same period, it appreciated.

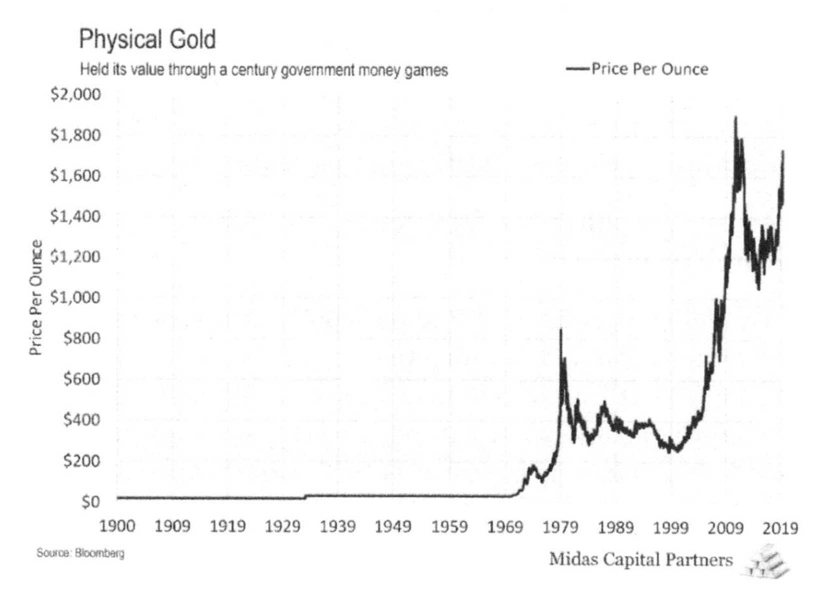

As we'll discuss in the following chapters, this century might be different. The threat of radical devaluation today is higher than ever before.

In the 20th century the U.S. won world wars. At one point it controlled roughly 60% of the official world gold supply. It patrolled the air, land, and seas of the planet.

Meanwhile, it ran what felt like serious budget shortfalls at the time. Even after losing two-thirds of its national gold reserves under the Bretton Woods agreement, it still held supremacy through the end of the century.

The strength to overcome these circumstances came from the U.S. economic engine. In the wake of each debt increase it generated higher GDP, and in turn, higher tax revenues. That engine shows signs of failure today. It takes increasingly large sums of debt to keep the economy afloat. Servicing that debt requires more debt.

Years ago, a small government deficit gave the economy a big boost. Today, giant deficits barely move the needle. As this power fades, debts mount up. Like a junkie, the government needs greater and greater piles of debt just to maintain its position. That's unsustainable.

Gold is the ultimate protection for what now looks inevitable.

In the following pages, I'll show you how the price of one gold ounce costs 500% more today than it did on January 1, 2000. That compares to a share of Warren Buffett's Berkshire Hathaway stock, which grew only 398% or the S&P 500 Index, which rose only 93% over the same period.

People say gold is boring, useless, without income, and even a barbarous relic of a bygone era. In the coming years, it might be your only chance to preserve the wealth that represents your life's work.

Part II – Why Now?

Introduction – It's Time to Be Realistic

After looking to the past, we're certain about two things. First, gold is money.

Over long periods of time it preserved, protected and often grew wealth like no other asset. It's liquid, meaning someone will buy it, even in the depths of depression.

Gold doesn't depend on another party for its worth. Bonds depend on a borrower to pay interest, stocks depend on companies to generate profits, apartments depend on tenants to pay rent. Gold depends on nothing. That makes it unique among all other assets. In the years to come that feature will prove to have inestimable value.

The second thing that's clear after looking to the past is governments have a bad habit of destroying the value of their money over time. Simply put, politicians can't resist spending tomorrow's savings today. The temptation is too great.

This has nothing to do with politics. Over long periods of time, right, left or center is irrelevant. Modern media drums up a circus to keep you distracted from seeing the main issue. Once you see the inevitable path ahead for modern money, you may lose interest in politics permanently.

Periods of fiscal restraint occasionally pop up. They usually follow economic turmoil or popular revolt. The public tends to watch over politicians more in the wake of a crisis. As time passes, memories fade. Slowly, governments always revert to their profligate ways.

Over thousands of years it's the same story. Just a little more borrowing seems reasonable. At times, it's the compassionate thing to do. Politicians whip up emotional stories to justify overspending. As we examine why now is the most critical time to shelter wealth from what's ahead, try to avoid falling prey to emotional distractions.

If you can do that, you'll see the financial system is not what you think. The old days of running a small deficit to foster growth are over. The entire system is in trouble. In the end, it won't be a crash that wipes people out. It will be a financial reset. This means a swift conversion to a new money system.

You won't get advanced notice about a financial reset. The reset only works if it happens when few expect it. The topics we cover in the coming section will help you spot the clues.

We'll expose the modern financial system for what it is. Like a swindler running a scheme, the stakes are so big today it takes enormous effort to maintain the façade. Forget about saving the structure beneath.

Borrowing today merely pays interest on previous borrowing. There's no hope of fiscal solvency. Central bankers make television appearances like financial celebrities. Years ago, people barely knew they existed.

As we get into the ugly truths about our financial system today, you'll need to let go of preconceived ideas. For instance, the U.S. is no longer a free market. We'll go over the evidence. You won't be able to take in the facts if you believe it's a free market simply because that's what you've been told.

Preconceived ideas might get you into a lot of trouble in the years ahead. Your wealth is on the line. That means your future is on the line. Let's get into why now may be your last chance to protect hard-earned wealth from an inevitable reset of the current financial system.

Chapter 10 – The System as You Know It Is Broken

On Monday morning August 19, 1991 every television set in the entire Soviet Union aired the same program. Changing the channel didn't help.

A beautiful rendition of Tchaikovsky's *Swan Lake* was a pleasant surprise, at first. The four-part ballet runs for about three hours. It ran over, and over, and over again for days.

There were a few brief interruptions. An unfamiliar anchorman came on to give spotty updates on the state of things in Moscow. President Gorbachev was ill, allegedly. But all would be well, enjoy the show.

The average Soviet citizen had no idea what was going on in Moscow. They'd later call it the "August Coup."

Over the prior weekend coup leaders locked Gorbachev in his Crimean vacation home. The ballet kept everyone distracted while plotters put the plan in motion.

In the end, it failed. However, four months later the USSR also failed. The coup was a warning sign of a major change ahead.

Major changes always give advance notice. The problem is most people don't pay attention. They either don't want to, or they can't. After change hits, they gripe and blame. Neither can restore the past.

For the average Soviet, 1991 was a confusing time. Something was going on, but many people didn't know exactly what.

The communist government controlled the media. That meant it controlled media messaging. Every government controls its domestic media. It realizes, wisely, that average people believe what they hear on television. They largely can't think for themselves. Hearing a message from a reporter with a credible appearance encourages trust.

When it comes to spotting change on the horizon a news anchor won't help. Worse, they'll tell you people talking about obvious change ahead are dangerous. The truth is, the only way to survive a big reset is to think for yourself. The clues appear in advance every time.

The first step in this process is looking back at the past. While the methods change, the general flow of events does not.

The next step is to take in the facts and tune out the media message. It's the commentary that gets people in trouble. It lulls them into complacency. They pass on the chance to act ahead of wealth-changing events.

Some Soviets saw change coming. There were signs. There was also an alternative to waiting until it was too late.

There was a robust underground economy in the Soviet Union. Premium goods and services lurked in the shadows. They changed hands in dollars. For those in the know, the dollar market offered some protection from wipeout.

The people I've met who remember watching *Swan Lake* for days admit they didn't understand the warning signs. Meanwhile, those who did positioned for change.

That change came when the Soviet system reset created a new class of wealth. Oligarchs emerged. Russia is a major economy today. Forget about its portrayal in the western media for a moment. We're interested in how to spot warning signs ahead of big change. We'll leave the politics to everyone else.

How the U.S. System Used to Work

We can't get into what's ahead for our wealth until we understand how the current system works. That is, how it used to work. Let's start with the basics.

Most governments get their funding from taxing activity within its borders. In the U.S., taxes on imports, exports, business profits and personal income make up most of its tax receipts.

That economic activity happening within a country's borders is its Gross Domestic Product (GDP). It's the total value of all goods and services produced in the country.

On average, the U.S. collects 16-18% of GDP in total tax revenue. Regardless of what personal tax rates are, the government rarely collects more or less than 16-18% of total economic activity.

GDP grew more than 90-fold between 1945-2020. Meanwhile, the percentage of GDP collected as taxes stayed about the same, as we can see in the next chart.

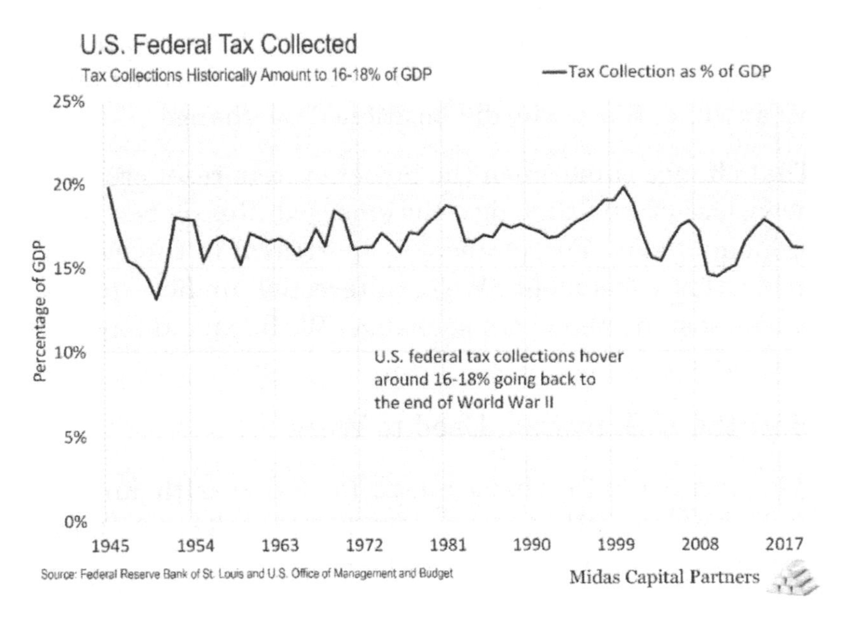

Higher GDP means higher tax revenue. That's why governments want GDP to grow. As that pie grows, the government's slice gets bigger.

In 2019 for instance, U.S. GDP was just under $21.5 trillion. The government collected $3.46 trillion in taxes that year. That's just over 16% of GDP.

U.S. Treasury Sells Bonds to Finance Overspending

The U.S. spent $4.45 trillion in 2019. That's almost $1 trillion more than it received in tax revenue.

It sells bonds to make up that $1 trillion shortfall.

The U.S. Treasury sells bonds, bills, and notes with maturity dates as short as four weeks and as long as thirty years. When they come due, it sells more. The U.S. debt pile never shrinks.

The next chart shows the total U.S. Treasury debt outstanding. You'll notice it tripled between 2005-2020.

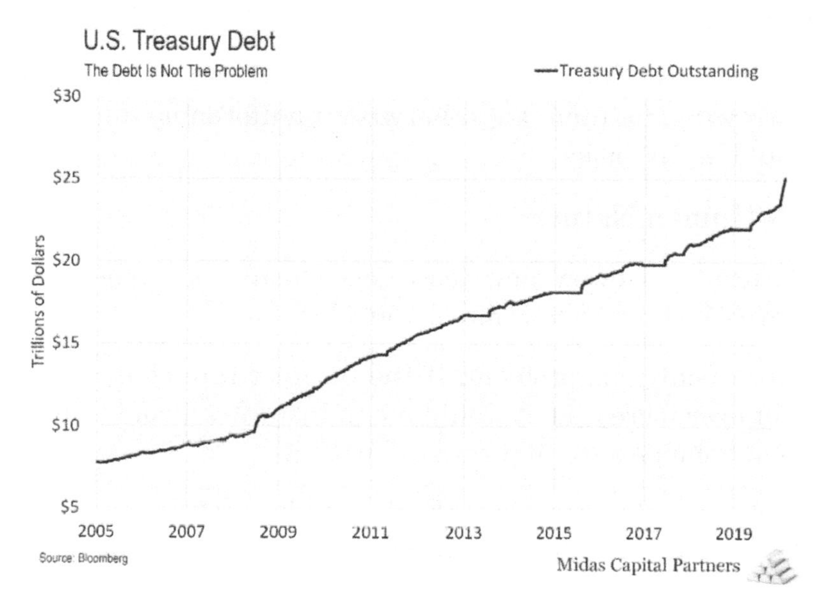

All of the debt sold by the U.S. Treasury carries the backing of the U.S. government. Specifically, the "full faith and credit" of the U.S. government. For more than a century, that's been a low-risk loan.

As of mid-2020 that debt pile topped $25 trillion. It will grow much larger. It's never been cheaper for the country to build a mountain of debt.

That's because interest on the debt is dirt cheap. The government pays less than 1% to borrow for as long as 10 years. It pays only 1.25% to borrow for 30 years. Where it once sold bonds, bills and notes to the free market, its own central bank buys many of them today. That keeps a lid on borrowing costs.

Imagine how many homes, cars, or businesses you could buy with a limitless supply of 1% credit. Take it one step further and imagine never having to repay the borrowed money. Each time a loan came due, you'd take out another loan to pay it off.

In this case, only a fool would sacrifice to pay off debt. Borrowing to fund an otherwise unaffordable lifestyle would be far easier.

It's Human Nature

Naturally, if every new loan gets cheaper and cheaper, there's no limit to how much you'd borrow.

There's only one problem. If the interest rate charged on debt ever increased, it would mean instant wipeout. You'd have to make sure that rate did not rise.

That's exactly what the U.S. does today. While it tripled the size of its debt pile, its interest expense barely budged.

You'd expect its interest expenses to also triple. That would be a normal consequence for any debt that tripled in size. But that's not what happened.

The U.S. benefits today from the lowest interest rates in recorded human history. That means looking back 2,000 years, it's never been cheaper to go on a borrowing binge.

Borrowing on this scale is not possible in a free market. In order to remain solvent, the U.S. has to suppress interest rates.

No Longer A Free Market

In Chapter 8, we discussed how fixing the price of oranges would punish premium orange growers while rewarding the worst growers. A free market produces the best oranges. The U.S. would never fix the price of oranges.

When it comes to interest rates, it's a different story. Interest rates are the price of money. There's nothing free about how that market works in the U.S. The same goes for most of the developed world today.

In a free market, buyers and sellers determine prices. The way this would work in a free market for interest rates is higher rates would attract more buyers looking for a good return on their money. Lower rates would be less appealing. The free market would find middle ground.

The problem is, if U.S. interest rates faced a free market the country would be insolvent overnight. That can't happen. So, the government does anything it has to do to keep interest rates as low as possible.

In the past, other countries bought U.S. bonds receiving market interest rates for a safe investment.

For instance, you'll hear people say, "The Chinese own us." Or, "We pay all that interest to China." In the 1980s it was Japan. Asserting that either will "own us" is way off base.

Japan holds about 5% of U.S. Treasury debt. It's the second largest holder. China is next with about 4% according to data from Bloomberg in May of 2020. That means the second and third largest holders of U.S. Treasury debt don't even make up 10% of the total.

Over the past 12 years the U.S. central bank, the Federal Reserve, bought up the majority of the country's debt. The Fed started out as a small buyer of U.S. debt. Today it's the majority holder. Soon it will be the entire market. That doesn't sound like a robust free market.

If U.S. interest rates faced a free market, they'd move to market prices. 0% doesn't sound like a return buyers and sellers would agree on.

That's why regardless of the costs, the U.S. government can't allow interest rates to rise.

Chapter 11 – No More Recessions

No one trusts a sales pitch that promises unlimited profits with no risk. There must be a catch.

It's normal for things to ebb and flow. That's how life works. That's how business works in a free market.

Recessions are the ebb in the natural ebb and flow of capitalism. You may notice the U.S. doesn't have recessions anymore. Instead, we have unusually long boom times interrupted by a crisis. A recession and a crisis are two different things.

Recessions were a necessary and normal part of a capitalist system. Crisis is part of a planned system, used to purge some participants while saving others. Sound familiar?

How Recessions Used to Work

Recessions worked like minor forest fires that burn back undergrowth.

If allowed to burn, these fires clear excess clutter and debris. They don't harm large trees protected with thick bark. When the smoke clears, green shoots appear as the first sign of new life. The fire creates fertile ground for growth. Then the cycle repeats.

For over 200 years this is largely how the U.S. system worked. Improving conditions build confidence. People take risks to expand their businesses. At some stage, undisciplined types take too much risk. They over-expand. Then there are too many businesses serving too few customers. Business slows. The weakest operators fail.

While this stings, it's the natural order of things in a capitalist system. The busted risktaker doesn't pay back the bank loan. The bank has to absorb the loss. The same goes for the landlord who leased space during the expansion. Everyone adjusts.

Penance is a key part of a recession. Not in the pious sense of the word. Penance in a recession means clearing the market of excess capacity.

Say a town has 50,000 residents and 5 tire shops. The local economy grows at a modest pace. People drive more. That means they need more tires. It's good times for the tire businesses in town. People notice. A few of them decide they'll get into the tire business too. They take out loans to open tire shops. The local bank makes the loan because the tire business looks good after a few years of steady growth. Now there are 10 tire shops.

Then comes a recession. Business slows. The local mill lays people off. Overall, people drive less. That means they don't need new tires as often. The tire business gets tough.

The weakest few tire stores close down. The first to go is the guy who borrowed too much to open his store. He spent heavily today with little regard for tomorrow. He borrowed to buy everything he now owns. Consequently, he can't handle one slow month. His store closes.

While this sounds insensitive, it's the most humane system in the economic world.

Just as fire naturally manages a forest, recessions thin out bad operators. The surviving stores grow more when business picks back up.

However, preventing natural fire means the forest undergrowth piles up so high the inevitable fire is uncontrollable. It ravages an area 10-times the size of the small blaze occasionally set by nature.

Crisis to Crisis

Without recessions the economy grows unchecked.

This might not sound like a problem. In the early days, it's not. The problems come later.

Think back to the early 2000s. After the September 11th attacks the economy entered recession. I remember the 2002 recession well. This was the last capitalist recession in the U.S.

At the time I had my first serious job out of college. The company I worked for borrowed heavily in the 1990s to finance a buyout. This was before my time. When business slowed in 2001 it could not afford the interest payments on its debt.

A Chicago-based competitor bought the firm for about 50-cents on the dollar. I joined the new management group charged with turning the business around.

Without the crippling debt, we helped the new owners ramp up the business and sell it for over $800 million several years later. That's more than four times what they paid creditors for the indebted business just before I started in 2003.

This is how things used to work. Borrowing too much during good times made it hard to survive a recession.

The 2002 recession was different. For the first time ever, the Federal Reserve went off-script. It stepped in to lower interest rates from 6.5% to 1% as shown in the next chart

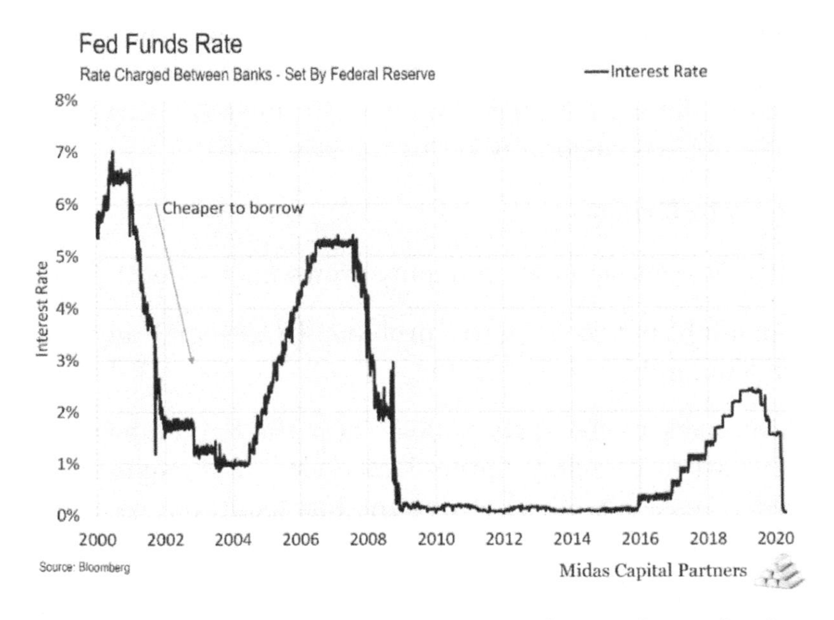

This meant the Fed made it cheaper for banks to lend to each other. The idea was banks in turn would lend to customers at lower rates. Customers would spend that newly loaned money. This would jumpstart the economy. It worked.

This happened for the first time on a grand scale across the entire U.S. financial system after the 2002 recession. Of course, some businesses failed. Not everyone had access to cheaper money.

Think back to our example of the tire stores during a recession. In the good times, many new stores opened.

They borrowed from local banks to get started. When business slowed, they struggled.

Imagine instead if the local bankers called the failing tire store and offered it lower interest rates. "Don't close up shop, we'll lower your interest rate from 6.5% to 1%." No one can resist that.

The problem is, it rewards bad behavior. The disciplined tire store owner who made prudent decisions running his business watches as his spendthrift competitor gets a lifeline.

Recession affects everyone. No business gets out unscathed.

Crisis on the other hand has selective effects. Some businesses get lifelines, others don't. Policymakers decide who to save.

Problems emerge over time as business owners change the way they take risks. Expecting lifelines after each crisis means they no longer think like capitalists.

The Consequence of Preventing Recession

Have you ever known a successful couple whose kid can't get it together? He's polished, well-educated, and certainly capable. But for some reason he can't get it into gear.

It's the same story every time. The parents are go-getters. They tell you all about what Junior should do next. Meanwhile Junior, smothered by these well-intentioned titans, hasn't developed any useful skills. Worse yet, he hasn't had any room for self-discovery.

There's an easy fix for this. The parents don't want to hear it. Cut Junior off entirely, immediately.

Subsidizing an unearned country club lifestyle neuters the entrepreneurial spirit. When problems arise, there are no skills to deal with them. Loving parents unintentionally prevented good potential from becoming great. The only way that happens is by experiencing life without a safety net.

When the Fed got involved in the 2002 recession it aimed to prevent the natural purging process that comes with recession. It took unnatural action to shorten it. That planted the seed of a massive speculative housing boom that ended in crisis.

Money moves like water flowing down a roof. Somehow, water always finds the lowest point. It travels down beams, under crevasses and through cracks. When it reaches the lowest point, there's nowhere else to go. Then it pools.

When the Fed lowered interest rates to an unnatural level in 2002 money flowed to profitable opportunities. Housing was one.

Cheaper money lent between the Fed and its banks slowly lowered mortgage rates. One percentage point at a time people refinanced loans over and over again.

Keep in mind, in a free market banks would set the mortgage rates based on risk factors. Instead, the Fed's falling borrowing costs kicked off a race to lend as much as possible regardless of creditworthiness.

The result, anyone who could fog a mirror took out a mortgage. Some people took out five of them. Then came what would have normally been a recession.

The Housing "Crisis"

I know how this played out firsthand.

In 2006 I had a trading partner. We shared all of our trading wins and losses, ideas, and thoughts about the market with each other. If you don't work for a major firm this is a good idea. It keeps your thinking sharp. It can also keep you out of trouble.

We both saw problems in the housing market. We sold short the stock of mortgage providers. This meant companies feasting on the mortgage boom. Technically speaking, we bet the market would notice the same problems we noticed and send these stocks tumbling.

That didn't happen until 2008. We quit on our bet in late 2006 as the stocks kept rising despite our conclusions. Then came the crisis.

Recessions are humane. Some people fail. However, anyone can save, work hard, and take prudent risks. With a little experience and hard work, it's not too hard to survive recession. Sure, there's sacrifice. But in the end that sacrifice pays off.

Crisis is different. Artificial excesses lead up to the crisis. In this case, lenders tripped over themselves to extend mortgage debt. Many lied on mortgage applications. They offered NINJA loans. NINJA stands for No Income, No Job, No Assets.

What the Fed did in 2002 set the stage for the housing boom and bust. It altered the free market function that makes capitalism what it is. Tampering with free markets created incentives for reckless lending.

NINJA loans don't happen in a capitalist system. No capitalist would take that kind of risk.

They don't lead to a normal recession. Instead, they trigger a collapse.

Crisis Breeds Chaos

With firsthand knowledge of how the housing boom and bust happened, I decided to become a landlord in 2009. It seemed like a once-in-a-lifetime opportunity to buy houses during a wholesale liquidation.

I saw the underbelly of the housing crisis. Entire city blocks boarded up. I didn't look at one house for sale that had an air conditioning unit. With the foreclosure process completed nobody lived in these houses. Filled with mildew, spiders and trash, bandits stripped them of everything from appliances to copper wire from the walls.

Crisis creates unique opportunities. I bought abandoned houses for as little as $10,000. This would never happen during a normal recession in a capitalist system.

Each time, I'd look up the court records and see the foreclosure judgment. On the $10,000 home it was $150,000. I bought another for $25,000 with a $250,000 foreclosure judgment.

People seem to love hearing about my buying spree. Truthfully, it was difficult to watch.

In the old days, banks chose borrowers wisely. If the mortgage went bad, it attended to the house until it sold to a more creditworthy borrower.

In 2008 every mortgage ended up as part of a giant investment pool with no attentive owner. The fevered pace of lending turned into millions of soured loans. With knee-high grass and boards on the windows whole neighborhoods looked abandoned.

The sales process for foreclosed homes was so chaotic I couldn't get agents to show them. Used to making six-figure incomes they had no interest in showing a $25,000 home. Most of them gave me the code to the lockbox on the front door. I'd submit a cash offer and either hear back in a week or not.

While this was a once-in-a-lifetime opportunity, it was a sign of what's to come. It was proof to me that capitalism ended a decade prior.

The 2008 crisis triggered some of the most radical monetary action in history. Crisis gave U.S. financial leaders the power to save some firms and purge others. That's a power that only comes with crisis. In a capitalist economy recession sorts things out naturally.

Crisis breeds chaos. It opens the door for more intervention. Nobody remembers the intervention that caused the crisis. With all eyes on the current crisis, emotions distract the public while financial leaders pick who survives and who crumbles.

The thing about a crisis is it builds and repeats until it wipes out the entire system. It leads to reset of the system. In the end, recession would have been a better option.

Chapter 12 – The Cure Is Worse Than the Disease

What's the problem with 0% interest rates?

Would you loan someone your life savings for a 0% rate of return?

Would you even bother building a "life savings?"

Or, would you spend every dollar on something you could enjoy today since waiting until tomorrow had no benefit?

Interest rates represent the price of money. In a capitalist system, people with money decide what to charge borrowers.

During times of serious economic stress, the cost to borrow naturally rises. In good times, there's plenty of money floating around which sends borrowing costs down.

This used to be how interest rates worked in the U.S. Not anymore.

The first time the Fed radically dropped interest rates from 6.5% to 1% it gave the economy a big boost. The idea was to encourage borrowing by making it cheaper to borrow. Newly borrowed money in turn would flow into the economy dulling the effect of recession.

The plan worked. Problem is, people bought things they didn't need. Extra houses, condos, cars, toys...it was a major boom. That unnatural boom helped shorten the 2002 recession. It improved the national mood.

Politicians Benefit from a Controlled Economy

There's almost always an American election around the corner. From congressmen every two years to the president every four and senators every six. Facing voters for reelection during a recession can be a nightmare.

During tough times every question at the town hall meeting is, "When are you going to help me get back to work?" It's as if politicians do the hiring and firing.

This isn't new. Going back thousands of years leaders knew a starving population led to trouble controlling the masses. When people get hungry, they attack.

A free market capitalist system means a recession might conflict with an election. Since recessions play out naturally, there's not much the politician can do. The only fair answer when asked when a recession would end is, "As soon as the economy clears out bad operators, growth will return naturally." This won't do.

The Fed's modern interventions into what was once a free market is a dream come true for politicians. It didn't start out this way. Initially, the central bank was an independent authority.

The idea for the Fed first emerged in the U.S. after the San Francisco earthquake of 1906. The quake set most of the city ablaze. A surge in insurance claims meant a flood of money rushing back into the western U.S. That caused turmoil in the currency markets.

Mostly based in London at the time, insurance firms sold or transferred gold to fund dollar-based insurance contracts in San Francisco. They needed so many dollars they sent the value of the dollar up dramatically causing a panic the following year. Known as, "The panic of 1907," it sparked calls for an independent U.S. central bank to oversee those money flows.

Fast forward 100 years and the bank is anything but independent. Politicians figured out downswings in the economy were tough. Just a little easing of credit conditions could help.

Bad Incentives Create Bubbles

In the summer of 2006, I took a weekend trip to Miami Beach. It was my first experience with what we later called the credit bubble.

I had dinner at a restaurant called Tantra on Washington Ave. It went out of business the following year. I'll never forget the scene.

After walking in the front door, I said, "Smells like a grass lawn in here." The hostess told me Tantra appeals to all the senses. Every day they laid fresh sod in the bar area to stimulate their guests' sense of smell.

The visual appeal of the place was obvious. Miami Beach is already a spectacle. Here it looked like they hired dozens of scantily clad models to parade around.

There was a bikini convention in town that weekend. One of the companies rented out the side dining room for a private party. It was incredibly chaotic.

Remember, I went to Tantra for dinner. The concierge suggested it and got me a table. He told me several times how lucky I was to get a table. The implication was he needed a tip for arranging it.

Finally, I sat down. Table for two next to the kitchen. Younger at the time, I cringed at the menu prices. The food was not great. Overall, it was a total bust. However, it was highly amusing.

Tantra doesn't work in a normal capitalist economy. Nobody uses hard-earned savings to lay fresh sod on the floor of a cocktail lounge every day. That only happens with borrowed money in the absence of consequences. This was a sign of what we now know was a credit bubble.

A bubble is what you get when you prevent natural capitalist forces from sorting out excesses in the economy. In short, when the money flows unnaturally it ends up in odd places.

The problem with credit bubbles is they grow large, then bust. If politicians publicly pressure the Fed for extra help to soften the pain of the bust, it plants the seeds of a larger bust to come.

Destroy the Incentives

In a crisis system, every bubble is bigger than the last. When it pops the mess is also bigger.

The final bubble will make a mess so large it triggers a financial reset. What that means is the pattern of bubble, crisis, bubble, crisis continues until everyone goes along with it assuming another bubble follows.

That means people get used to the pattern. The final bubble explodes and there's no more steam left in the system. It resets. The price of everything converts to a new value under the new money system. It happens overnight. At that point it's too late to prepare.

Today, your incentive is to not prepare. Preparing means spending less than you earn, putting aside the difference for tomorrow.

Meanwhile, the instant there's a sign of trouble the Fed and the government step in with a rescue plan. They have the power to pick survivors and set the terms. Try to see the pattern. It's right in front of you, if you care to look.

The excesses of the 2006-2007 credit bubble hit extreme levels triggering the 2008 bust. Nobody remembered the 2002 recession and the cheap credit created to artificially kick the economy back into gear.

In the 2008 crisis, 158-year old Lehman Brothers failed almost overnight. Entire city blocks had boards on the windows. Stocks crashed 57% from their 2007 high. It was a bloodbath.

Meanwhile, financial news media ran wall-to-wall coverage of the crisis. Every story was a prediction of the next firm to fail. Insurance companies, auto manufacturers, pensions, banks, all teetered on the brink. Again, no mention of the decisions earlier in the decade that set the stage for the crisis.

Instead of letting the dust settle naturally – letting prudent firms survive and others fail – politicians urged the Fed to rescue the system. They said the world as we knew it would crumble if they didn't intervene.

Each crisis paves the way for a new extreme in Fed money games. There's a tolerance to what worked last time. It takes something slightly bigger and more dramatic. Otherwise there's no effect.

$50 billion was a controversial sum needed to bailout the now forgotten Mexican debt crisis in the 1990s. $700 billion was controversial in September 2008. In 2020, $2.8 trillion is not enough to ease the effect of the virus-related economic shutdown.

If the Fed and its co-conspirators spoke in plain language, they'd face pitchforks. That's not going to happen. Instead, they use carefully worded statements to discuss the rescue plan for each crisis situation.

These Orwellian word games work well. They distract people so thoroughly they almost forget there's a crisis.

Get Used to Alphabet Soup

There's a trick to deceiving people. George Orwell described it in his dystopian novel *1984*.

Orwell showed how controlling speech controls behavior. Done effectively, the society evolves in the direction you send it.

Today, the Fed and the government use acronyms to disguise the meaning of financially destructive actions. Acronyms sound important and credible. They change the way people talk about an organization or institution. After a while, it becomes familiar to talk about an acronym without questioning its legitimacy.

They also carefully chose the names of laws. The names appeal to the heart, not the head. They have emotional appeal while masking draconian language inside.

For example, The Food Safety Act makes it virtually impossible for smaller farms to succeed. It's a greenlight for agribusiness, which is arguably far more dangerous than local produce.

Acronyms also appeal to emotions. Take the CARES Act for instance. Coronavirus Aid, Relief, and Economic Security Act. That sounds like something good, compassionate, supportive. Do a little digging and find the original bill, introduced a full year earlier, had a different name.

The bills, laws, programs of all scopes and sizes have hundreds of billions of dollars tucked in every corner. The CARES Act gave payments of $1,200 to citizens earning less than $75,000. Those payments totaled 15% of the legislation. The other 85% or $1.8 trillion went to thousands of companies, states, hospitals, universities, all financed by more government borrowing.

This careful naming works well as cover for excessive money creation. If you called it what it is, people wouldn't stand for it.

In 2008 the Fed unveiled TARP. That sounds like something practical. Something that might keep you out of the elements on a camping trip.

This TARP was the "Troubled Asset Relief Program" designed to absorb at full price the soured loans left over from the 2002-2006 credit bonanza. Not every firm got a bailout however. Lehman Brothers, for instance, didn't make the cut.

Notice when we call it a bailout, it sounds bad. When we say Lehman "wasn't eligible for TARP" it sounds like there were stringent requirements unmet by one bad actor.

Treasury Secretary Hank Paulson at the time said the exclusion of Lehman wasn't personal. His decades of competing with Lehman as CEO of rival Goldman Sachs didn't affect his decision. Regardless, Washington had the power to choose who survived.

After the $700 billion TARP came "QE" or Quantitative Easing. This phrase literally did not exist prior to the Fed branding it as something helpful and necessary. These two words bolted together disguise its true purpose.

Using initially a modest $600 billion to buy mortgage-related bonds from certain banks, QE sounded like a stabilization mechanism. Nobody wants things to be unstable. However, no one bothered to connect the dots. The banks selling these bonds to the Fed were often the same ones that created the instability in the first place.

Remember, the housing market boomed with the advent of NINJA loans (No Income, No Job, No Assets) and loose underwriting standards. At the first sign of trouble these underwriters vanished. After raking in fees for years the major banks risked going under, crippled by the weight of bad loans.

The Fed's QE program bailed them out as shown in the next chart. It got the plumbing of the financial system flowing again. By June of 2010 the Fed had around $2.1 trillion worth of mortgages, bank debt and Treasury bonds. It paused its QE support in June. The market nearly tumbled.

In August 2010, about sixty days later, the Fed launched QE2. This was a second round of Quantitative Easing. Remember, this is a second round of a word that had no literal meaning.

When QE2 wrapped up, the market started to tumble. So, the Fed launched QE3 in 2012 saying it would buy $40 billion of Treasury bonds per month indefinitely.

In the middle of all this the Fed kicked off "Operation Twist." This meant it could sell certain bonds and buy others to make interest rates resemble a healthy economy. I know it's confusing. You wonder how the Fed itself keeps it straight.

Later came "Tapering" where the Fed promised to return things to normal by getting rid of some of the bonds it owned. That's impossible. The U.S. central bank is so intertwined in its financial markets, it is the market.

The scope and scale of its involvement in what used to be free markets will never decrease. If it did, the system would collapse.

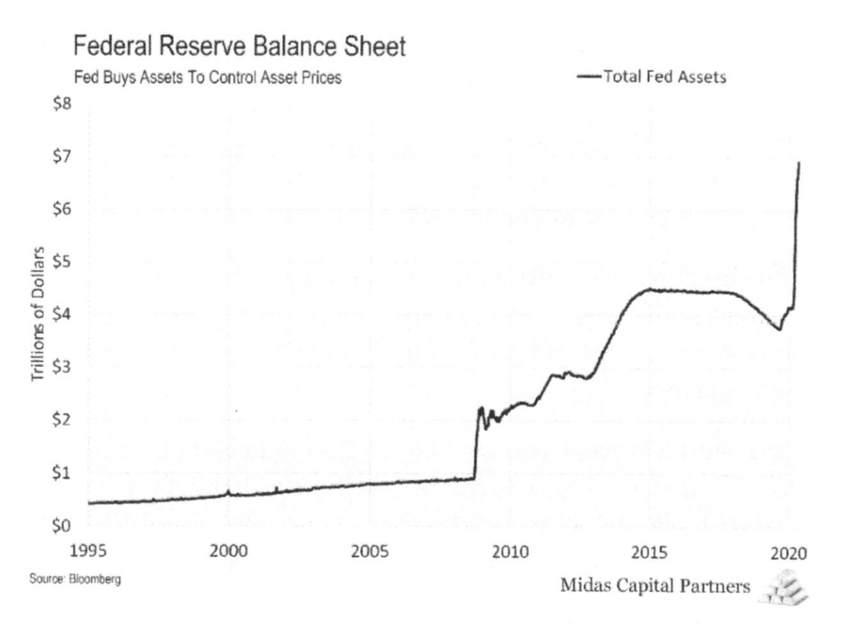

The Fed held over $7 trillion worth of financial assets on its books as of May 2020. U.S. Treasury debt makes up more than 50%. Mortgage debt about 25%.

The Fed's balance sheet is nine-times larger than before the 2008 crisis. Every measure implemented is temporary, essential, and in the best interest of saving the system. Each time it slows the pace of expansion, markets tremble. The path from $7 to $10 trillion won't take long.

Keep in mind, the value of all the gold ever mined in the world is about $10 trillion today. There's no scrambled acronym that can produce more gold. The supply grows slowly. It's an indestructible store of wealth in a time of destructive money and credit creation.

Unlike the supply of gold, the Fed can create as many U.S. dollars as it needs. As long as the rest of the world accepts them, there's no limit to growth.

Interest Rates Will Never Rise

As with all government action, artificially lowering interest rates was billed as a temporary measure. Manipulation is never temporary.

It's the same as telling one lie, then another to cover it up. Before you know it, you're spending all day keeping track of these lies making sure nobody gets the wrong story. It's exhausting.

Lowering interest rates to 1% in 2002 staved off recession. After rates rose to just over 5% by 2006 the Fed lowered them back to 0% at the first sign of trouble. More borrowing softened the blow of the 2008 crisis.

After 2008 the Fed left rates near 0% for roughly eight years. Again, pinning rates at 0% was a temporary measure. If eight years is temporary, I'd like to see permanent.

Finally, in 2018 rates crept up to 2%. At one time 2% was paltry. Now it was sky high. The walls started shaking. The financial system ran into trouble. The S&P 500 Index fell 20% between late September and Christmas Eve.

See this for what it was. It's an important warning sign of what's to come for the U.S. system. It's also proof this is not a free market. And if it's not a free market, the value of free market assets like stocks, bonds and real estate are in trouble.

Sustained rock-bottom interest rates created a feeding frenzy for asset managers. An unnatural force pinned interest rates at 0%. Big fund managers could borrow immense sums to make bets on low interest rates. This was easy money.

With the Fed keeping interest rates unnaturally low, rates on everything else would surely follow. Rates on corporate bonds for instance fell and fell. When the interest rate on a bond falls that means the price of those bonds rises.

Fund managers bought bonds hand over fist. It wasn't due to renewed confidence in the fundamentals of the underlying company. It was due to the Fed's unnatural involvement in the debt market. Even junk bonds shot to new highs minting fortunes not possible in a market free of intervention.

At the first sign of increase, things got tight. After years of easy money, billionaire hedge fund managers like Ray Dalio of Bridgewater Associates called for the Fed to stop raising interest rates. Remember, we're talking about 2% after eight years at 0%.

Dalio said it best. In November of 2018 he told CNBC the Fed action was, "hurting asset prices." That's trouble for his, at the time, $18.1 billion fortune which he earned managing Bridgewater's $160 billion in investment assets.

I have no problem with Dalio earning big bucks. He deserves it. He played the game properly. He'd be a fool not to pressure the Fed for more of what butters his bread.

The issue is, rates will never rise. If they do, the U.S. system crumbles. That triggers a dramatic financial reset. Dalio will be fine. Complacent savers won't.

This brings us back to our initial question. Are you happy with a 0% return on your hard-earned wealth? I doubt it.

Don't let the 0% interest rates distract you from the core issue. The U.S. is not a free market. There are implications.

Stocks are a free market phenomenon. There's no stock market in Cuba. There's no free market for anything. It's a controlled system where the ruling party picks winners. Believe me, there are winners.

One of my close friends is Cuban. I've been to Havana with him several times. He's connected there, which means life is good.

He explained the process of buying property recently. There's no real defense of title. Meaning, you can buy it, and you own it, but down the road you might not own it. That means, you don't own it.

Let's be clear, I am not suggesting the U.S. could devolve to the level of an agrarian, Communist, island nation.

What I am saying is the absence of a free market means it's time to rethink your assets. Do you want stocks in a market that's not free? They don't function on fundamental free market pricing. Some win, some lose. You better choose wisely.

Do you want to own real estate in a market that's not free? Tenants stop paying rent due to a possible virus outbreak. Forbearance measures prevent eviction for months. Meanwhile, you're on the hook for mortgage payments if you want to keep the property.

Then you've got property taxes. The bloated city budget needs your support. You can't move the property. You might suffer a year or two of negative cash flow. Doesn't sound so exciting.

This Is a One-Way Street

0% interest rates will never rise in a meaningful way. If they do, the entire system breaks.

Not only will they not rise, they'll eventually go negative. When you face charges for holding money at the bank, you'll withdraw it and spend. That stimulates growth desperately needed by indebted companies and a government starved for tax revenue.

At the slightest sign of rising interest costs today the financial media, fund managers, and even the President apply public pressure to the Fed. They all know what would happen if rates did rise.

In a free market, lenders ask a lot of questions before funding a loan. With interest rates pegged at 0% any loan is profitable. That fuels a lending bonanza. It also creates "zombie companies."

A zombie company can't generate enough revenue to service its debt. That means it can only survive with more debt.

In 2019, ten years into a booming economic expansion, CNN Money reported 13% of companies in advanced economies were zombies. In 1980 the number was 2%.

Zombie firms immediately go bankrupt without access to greater and greater supplies of debt.

This is not about no-name firms peddling junk products. Major corporations borrow big to fund dividends, stock buybacks and acquisitions.

In an April 2020 Forbes article contributor Frank Holmes of U.S. Global Investors cited $9.6 trillion of outstanding corporate debt for U.S. firms. That excludes financial companies. Meaning, these are the firms that make the products, transport us, and keep life on track.

Companies borrowed big at low interest rates. Every 1% increase to that $9.6 trillion means $96 billion in additional interest expense.

That's a big blow to profits. In some cases, it wipes them out entirely. That boosts the ranks of the zombie firms.

This means if the U.S. allowed rates to find their free market levels set by actual buyers and sellers of bonds, many companies wouldn't make it.

That in turn means they'd enter bankruptcy, their bonds often selling for pennies on the dollar. Remember, in a rigged market the Fed sets the price. In a free market the one with the cash sets the price.

We'll never see that market again. As we barrel towards an inevitable financial reset, it's time to protect hard-earned wealth.

Chapter 13 – Paying People Not to Work

"Free cash greases the wheels of the economy." That's according to Rutger Bregman, author of the book *Utopia for Realists.*

Bregman advocates giving every person a baseline monthly income. Regardless of skill level, effort, schooling, or behavior, everyone gets a monthly stipend.

He tells mashable.com once receiving a monthly stipend, "People buy more, and that boosts employment and incomes." He says this guaranteed income gives people the "individual freedom" needed to quit their current job if they hate it. This fosters the creative spirit.

Bregman might sound like a radical. He's not. The concept of paying people not to work is already in place.

Not So Radical

During the virus panic of early 2020 a friend of mine got a call from his CPA. "I want you to hire everyone you can, your mom, aunt, uncle, anyone with a social security number…do it today."

A successful entrepreneur, he told the CPA these people don't have the skills to add any value to his advertising business. The CPA explained he needed to show a big payroll to get as much "PPP money" as possible before it ran out.

PPP is the Payroll Protection Program. Part of the CARES Act, the PPP loans employers as much as 2.5-times their normal monthly payroll expense. The loan carries an interest rate of 1%. At the end of the year the government will review the loan and potentially turn it into a grant. According to the CPA, it's easy money.

There's no such thing as a PPP in a free market. My friend is a free market entrepreneur. From his perspective, businesses succeed by meeting the needs of customers. You can only do that with excellent people. He'd never hire his distant relative who knows nothing about advertising.

Everyone knows this is true when it comes to products. Some are just better than others. For instance, I enjoy a great cup of coffee. It takes more work to produce a great cup of coffee. The shop I like has an artisanal roasting process. It's completely different from the self-serve coffee at the gas station. I'll pay more for it because it's great.

Wine drinkers know all about this. Rare varietals, expertly processed and aged to perfection, sell for high prices because they're the best.

People want the best. They want you to see that they have the best. Even in a suburban community where every home looks the same people go to great lengths to show they have something better than their neighbor.

No dinner party host has friends over and announces she'll serve average beef with an average bottle of wine. Imagine sitting in that average house looking at average art wondering what you're doing there.

The whole concept of average only exists if there's a top and bottom. You don't know something is below average unless there's an above average. People understand this when it comes to food and wine. They struggle when it comes to individuals.

Everyone Is not Equal

While we all look similar, two arms and legs etc., we're not equal.

My friend with the advertising agency and his staff are not equal. I remember when he started the agency ten years ago. He couldn't take it anymore slaving away at a large corporate agency. So, he used his credit card to buy a laptop. He risked it all to start his own one-man agency. A decade later, he's a multimillionaire.

He respects his staff. They're all smart. But not one of them helped him start the agency. There's a chance one of them will quit and start a competing agency one day. But at this time, he's the big boss because he took the biggest risk.

In a free market the risktakers who succeed reap the benefits. With several houses, a beautiful farm, numerous vehicles and plenty of savings, my friend's big bet on himself paid off.

That's why it's hard to hear the CPA explain that he needs to hire a bunch of very nice but unskilled relatives in order to get the PPP money. That PPP money flows into the PPPLF (Paycheck Protection Program Lending Facility) and once it's gone, there's no more free money.

The whole thing doesn't make sense to people who think about it too much. Don't think about it. The answer is obvious. Rutger Bregman's income for all is already here.

The PPP loan means businesses like my friend's advertising agency continue paying workers while they stay home during a virus quarantine. The quality of work coming out of these homebound workers is not equal.

Some use a spare bedroom and keep regular hours. Some work more. Others work as little as possible. Nobody knows what's really happening because nobody can see. But the pay stays the same regardless, in order to get the PPP loan.

The PPP loans were part of The CARES Act. That also boosted unemployment compensation. Normally computed at the state level, the federal government added an extra $600 per week for the unemployed.

$600 per week means an extra $15/hour for the unemployed. That's straight from Washington, and on top of the state unemployment payments. Ironically, the federal payment of $15/hour is the number floated as a basic wage.

Basic wages are yesterday's news. That concept implies paying workers a minimum of $15/hour for actual labor. This new program pays $15/hour to people who don't work.

People hear this and immediately say, "some people need more help in challenging times." Oh? I thought we were all equal. Now you say some people aren't equal, they need more help. Which one is it?

The whole thing is a farce. Call it what you want, PPP, PPPLF, CARES, it's all the same. Acronyms and controlled language mask the real message. We'll pay people not to work across the board soon.

Who Pays the People Not Working?

Fast forward to Bregman's utopian society where nobody takes a job they don't enjoy. Imagine how people spend their day.

Maybe they take a bike ride, assuming someone enjoys building concrete bike paths for them. Every city would need people who enjoy trash collection, sewage treatment, and other tasks required in modern life.

In my early teens I had a job in my father's furniture warehouse. It's an old tobacco warehouse. In the summer it feels like what I imagine the face of the sun must feel like. Plus, furniture comes in huge cardboard boxes. They create a lot of dust. By 10:00 AM you're drenched in sweat and discolored from dust.

Nobody would choose to do that job over a free stipend. Therefore, nobody would unload, receive, and reload furniture for delivery. All the people sitting at home playing video games during the workday would have to come get the boxed furniture themselves.

Let's say there are 200 million working people in the country. If we pay those people $2,000/month all year that's $24,000 as a basic income. Multiplied by 200 million and that's $4.8 trillion which Bregman says will produce "individual freedom."

The total size of the U.S. economy now is about $21.5 trillion. That's all the goods and services produced in a year. That means all we have to do is tax every cent of commercial activity by 22.5% and we've got it covered. Sounds easy.

Well, we've also got the rest of the government to fund. Surely, we need soldiers, assuming they don't mind fighting. We also need highway workers, I guess. Then there's maintenance staff, safety people, we probably still need some government administrators to dole out the free money.

Of the $4.4 trillion in 2019 government spending, I'm not sure what we'd cut. So now we're up to just under half of GDP. All we need to do is assess a 45% tax on all commercial activity, and we should be OK.

The concept here is Universal Basic Income (UBI). You'll hear more about it. That's how these things work. First, float a crazy idea. Next, give it an acronym that sounds useful. Then use a crisis to slip in the first taste of it to get people hooked. Ten years into it they'll have no clue how they got into this tangle.

Meanwhile, remember that the cost of paying people not to work is infinite. It fights human nature on every front. We both know it won't work. Trying it means unlimited spending. That means another radical increase in borrowing.

We know federal debt grows until there's so much it smothers the economy below. With that engine smothered it's hard to hold on to wealth through traditional means. Stocks don't keep up because business struggles. Bonds produce a small return but the loss of purchasing power more than eats it up. It's essential to own something that benefits from the inevitable situation as it unfolds.

Remember, while debt grows without limit, the gold supply tends to grow at around 1.5% per year. It takes immense stress and strain to produce gold. That's after a prospector takes excessive risks to look for, discover, and define the potential gold mine. This is a decade-long process at best.

That's why there's only $10 trillion worth of gold above ground today. Compare that to world debt which started 2020 over $250 trillion and may finish closer to $300 trillion.

The total world gold supply is so small it fills roughly three Olympic size swimming pools. Keep in mind, that's after mining for thousands of years.

Gold's limited supply is the ultimate wealth protection in a world of limitless money creation.

Chapter 14 – Negative Interest Rates

Imagine receiving this note from your local bank.

Dear Valued Customer,

Effectively immediately, the interest rate on all account balances greater than $10,000 will be -1%. We will calculate interest based on your daily balance and assess the interest charge on the last business day of your statement cycle. Any balance under $10,000 will receive our standard 0% interest.

We appreciate your business and loyalty!

Sincerely,

Your Local Banker

Consider what this means. On a surplus $100,000 account balance you'd lose $1,000 per year.

The concept is negative interest rates. While this might sound impossible, it already exists.

There are more than $11 trillion worth of government bonds across the world with interest yields below 0%

today. At one point in 2019 there were more than $17 trillion worth as the next chart shows.

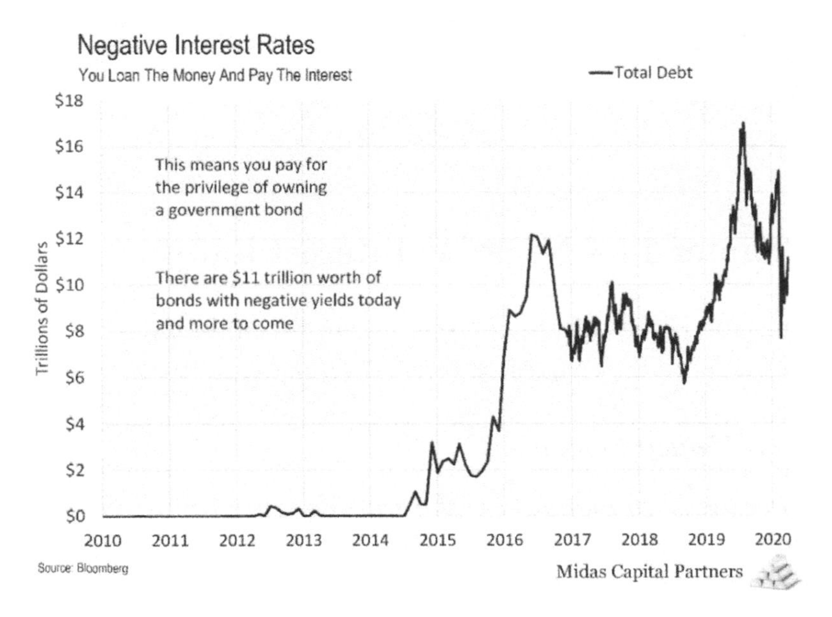

Japan had $5.8 trillion worth of negative yielding government bonds outstanding as of June 2019 according to Bloomberg. To be clear, this means the bond buyer pays the Japanese government a premium to own a bond.

I know this is new for most people so let's make sure we're on the same page. In the old days you bought a government bond for $1,000 that carried a 5% coupon (annual interest). Twice a year you'd get a check for $25 representing a total annual interest payment of $50. When the bond matured, you'd get a check for your last interest payment and the $1,000 face value. This is how bonds worked in the old days.

The bonds we're talking about today, all $11 trillion of them, effectively work backwards. Assuming the same conditions as mentioned above, you'd buy a $1,000 government bond for $1,050. Assuming the bond matures one year later, the government would return $1,000. That means you paid the government 5% for the privilege of owning its bond. This is how negative interest rates work.

It's not just Japan. France, Germany, Spain, and even some U.S. companies had negative yielding debts outstanding in mid-2019. There will be more.

Why the Fed Would Mandate Negative Interest Rates

For most people, the first instinct during turbulent times is to hoard cash. This doesn't always mean physical paper cash as much as it means bank deposits.

It's hard to amass much physical cash. The $100 bill is the largest denomination today. There hasn't been a larger U.S. bill printed since 1945. The last $500, $1,000, $5,000 and $10,000 bills went out of circulation in 1969.

Unless you run a criminal enterprise chances are slim you'll hold more than $10,000 or $20,000 in physical cash. If you do, it's the exception not the norm.

Most of your cash ends up in money market funds. This is by design.

Remember, money market funds used to pay interest. They loaned to reputable companies for short periods. They passed that interest to you as the depositor. That doesn't happen anymore. At least, in an amount that has consequence.

Even so, when the walls of the economy rattle, people still shove cash into money market funds and other accounts that used to be safe havens. The next chart shows how the total quantity of money on deposit in these accounts surged during each of the 2002, 2008, and 2020 crisis periods.

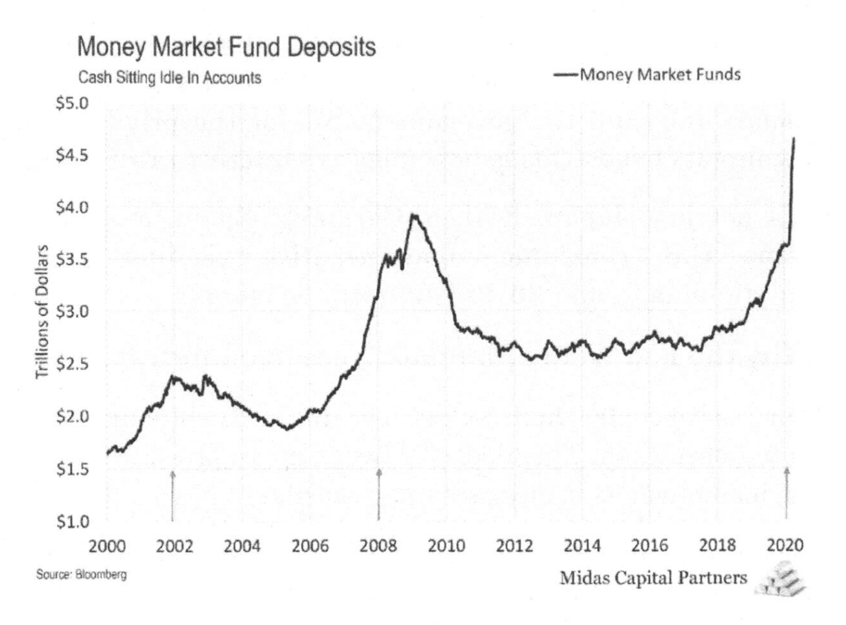

That's bad news for the Fed. Remember, it's trying to keep interest rates pinned at 0% while keeping tons of cash flowing through its member banks. When you pull your cash aside to wait for the dust to clear, you make the Fed's job more difficult.

Soon the Fed's interventions won't work at all. 0% rates can't make money any cheaper. However, negative rates can.

Depositors Would Stimulate the Fatigued System

Next time, you will fix the financial system.

Remember, in 2019 bond buyers held $17 trillion worth of negative-yielding government debt. That means they paid to own it. Imagine what the other investment options look like if the best choice is paying the borrower to take your money.

At the next sign of crisis, you'll respond as usual shoving all your surplus savings, emergency funds, and retirement into money market funds. Then, you'll get that letter from your bank.

Next, you'll try moving your money to a different bank. Same situation. Banks won't have a choice here.

Banks earn money through what's called the Net Interest Margin (NIM). This is the difference between the rate they pay savers and the rate they charge borrowers.

For instance, if savers earn 1% on deposits and borrowers pay 5% the bank has a NIM of 4%. This NIM spread doesn't change much outside of efficiencies and cost-cutting efforts. It can only go so low.

As lending rates fall towards 0% banks can't function. They need a cheaper source of funds. Deposit rates are already close to 0% now at most local banks. In order to stay in business, they may have to go negative.

Out of options, you'd do the next logical thing. Pull your money out and put it to work somewhere else.

Maybe you'd buy real estate. If it earned a 1% yield, you'd figure that's better than paying 1% to let it sit.

Maybe you'd buy stocks. There might be a 2% dividend yield, again better than the bank.

In both cases there are risks. Real estate constantly depreciates. The roof, paint, plumbing, appliances... there's always a need for maintenance. That costs money. It would eat into your returns.

Plus, you won't be the only one searching for a deal.

There were $4.75 trillion worth of money market fund deposits in the U.S. as of May 2020 according to data from the Investment Company Institute (ICI). If negative interest rates pushed even half that idle cash into real estate, it would send prices higher. That in turn means lower expected returns.

The same goes for stocks. Stocks go up when there are more buyers than sellers. Trillions sitting idle in money funds could light a spark under stock prices regardless of worsening market fundamentals.

You Did the Fed's Bidding

By taking your idle savings out of bank accounts and rushing to invest it, you did what the Fed failed to do.

$4.75 trillion, or some portion of it, shoved into the economy kickstarts things. It gives the Fed one more crisis, bubble, crisis, bubble cycle. Maybe more if you don't catch on quickly.

This is a dangerous game. It's your hard-earned wealth that's on the line. The investments we're talking about come with risk. At some stage, you want to reduce risk and live your life. And you don't want to pay interest to do it.

Gold always receives harsh criticism for being a 0% yielding asset.

Warren Buffet chided the metal as useless. He said after digging it out of the earth you, *".... melt it down, dig another hole, bury it again and pay people to stand around guarding it. It has no utility. Anyone watching from Mars would be scratching their head."*

Which sounds crazier, gold or negative interest rates?

Chapter 15 – Administrative Measures

Imagine it's a normal Sunday night at 7:00 PM.

You see a notification on your smartphone, an email from your bank, and a text from an informed friend all within a few minutes. Your bank will not open Monday morning.

The email from the bank is friendly. It cites a Federal Reserve statement that banks across the country will not open on Monday. There's no need to worry. This is merely a "bank holiday."

Logically, you drive to an ATM to get some cash. There's a line of cars. The machine has a bank holiday message limiting withdrawals. Try another bank, same thing. You'll have to get by on the cash you have or credit and debit cards.

The next day, every major financial news outlet covers the bank holiday. The stock market opens like normal. You can buy and sell stocks but cannot wire cash out of your account. Things seem somewhat normal.

That night the President and the Federal Reserve Chairman make a joint statement about the bank holiday. Media outlets repeated the phrase "bank holiday" so many times it started to sound normal.

A holiday sounds like a vacation. While it's a wise choice of words on the government's behalf, this is not the kind of vacation you want to go on.

As the press conference ramps up it's clear there is a major problem. The Fed Chairman explains how "rogue states" conspired to damage the market for U.S. Treasury bonds with coordinated selling. He called the selling an "attack."

He explains that the Treasury bond market is the key mechanism the government uses to fund itself. It must borrow to fund a gigantic budget deficit. That means its spending is far in excess of revenues from tax collection. Any rise in interest rates renders the government insolvent.

The President steps in and says we can't allow these bad actors to hurt the U.S. He goes on about the elderly needing medication and hungry children. He blames it all on foreign states. There's no mention of decades of borrowing to fund government overspending.

The bank holiday puts the aggressors on their heels. That's the storyline of course.

The truth is, the U.S. government debt load became so large it crippled its economic engine. Like a business that runs up $5 of debt for every $1 in sales, it can't go on forever. Nobody wants to buy U.S. Treasury bonds anymore.

To fix the last crisis the Fed ushered in negative interest rates. People decided to spend their savings avoiding paying the government for the privilege of buying its bonds. That pumped up the economy blowing an even bigger bubble. Then the Fed was out of options.

The good news is, the bank holiday will end in a few days. The bad news is any account balance in excess of the FDIC deposit insurance limit will automatically be converted into U.S. Treasury bonds yielding -1%.

In the real world we'd call this theft, or at least a government seizure. It would surely violate some constitutional right. Not anymore. Constitutional rights take a backseat during times of crisis.

Wisely, the Fed and Treasury would carefully choose the name for this seizure. It needs to sound important, formal, and beyond scrutiny. They'll call it, "Administrative Measures."

You Think This Can't Happen?

Think again.

It can certainly happen in the U.S. It already happened in the European Union in 2013.

Without advance notice, depositors in the Mediterranean island nation of Cyprus, an E.U. member, lost access to their bank accounts. They could wait in line to use the ATM. However, there was a €100 daily withdrawal limit.

This was a bank holiday at first. It turned into seizure of any deposits in excess of €100,000.

Several years prior Cyprus attracted large inflows of bank deposits. Its banks offered high interest rates to lure money in. That money in turn went to work in the country's financial system. The island nation boomed.

The economic boom also boosted tax revenues. The local government sold bonds to finance additional spending in excess of tax revenues. Remember, governments can't help themselves when it comes to spending tomorrow's tax revenue today.

In 2012 Cyprus ran into some trouble. The nearby Greek debt crisis created panic. Cyprus struggled to sell bonds. Unable to borrow more it stood ready to default.

Any government can spend in excess of tax revenues as long as someone buys its bonds. That's the government equivalent of taking a loan to live beyond its means. It works well until it doesn't. Eventually bond investors sour and turn away. That's when it's all over in an instant.

When that day came, E.U. leaders concocted a "bail in" scheme already outlined in its legal code. A bail in works like a bail out except for one major difference. Where a bail out is a financial lifeline provided by government with the final bill passed to taxpayers, bank customers fund the bail in.

Anyone holding more than the deposit limit of €100,000 would contribute to the stabilization effort. Think of this as a bank robbery in reverse. Instead of a rogue customer holding up the bank, the bank holds up the customers.

€100,000 (USD$110,000) might sound like a lot of money. Soak the rich. The problem is, plenty of small businesses, retirees, or people saving for a big purchase have that in a bank account at some time in their adult life. In those cases, the seizure meant a financial wipeout.

A group of 676 customers who lost large deposits took up an unsuccessful legal action against the country, and its banks. They suffered a collective $135 million loss in the seizure.

Before you write off Cyprus as an island nation only suitable for vacations (not bank holidays) consider this. It enacted the bail in measures under a European Union directive. That means the government and the banks acted legally in seizing customer deposits.

This Can Happen in the U.S.

To be clear, I didn't think up the idea of "Administrative Measures" myself. A European friend told me about it. A friend of his who works at the French Ministry of the Economy and Finance bragged to him that this legislation was in the drawer and ready to go if needed in a future crisis.

The action makes so much sense from the government's perspective. It knows people hoard bank deposits during a crisis. In mid-2020 there was more than $4.75 trillion sitting idle in U.S. money market funds. If it struggles to sell debt, seizing that idle money is a logical fix.

Administrative measures aren't the first domino to fall though. These things work in succession. Throughout history government action becomes progressively more desperate as the end nears.

The U.S. Federal Reserve has several cards left to play before implementing a forced purchase of Treasury bonds in a scheme like administrative measures.

Each action seems unprecedented at first. Later it seems ineffective. To stay inflated the market needs more and more dramatic actions.

After the U.S. government bought nearly $7 trillion worth of mortgage and Treasury debt in an effort to peg interest rates at 0%, that action lost its effect on markets by 2020. That's why by mid-2020 the Fed for the first time started buying junk bonds. These are bonds issued by companies likely to go bust at the first sign of trouble. They usually carry high rates of interest to compensate buyers for the unusually high-risk profile. In order to prevent a credit crisis, the Fed stepped in as a major buyer.

The Fed may also begin buying stocks. This would prevent the stock market from going down. With the power to create unlimited amounts of currency, it could easily stabilize the $30 trillion U.S. stock market by stepping in as a buyer.

Before you think it's crazy to imagine the Fed buying stocks, consider that the Swiss National Bank and the Central Bank of Japan bought large stock portfolios over the past few years.

In the case of Japan, the Central Bank bought so many of its bonds it could no longer affect the market with purchases. It then started buying stocks. Today, it's among the largest holders of Japanese stocks.

If things continue at their current pace, the Fed could run into the same dilemma.

After buying up most of the Treasury bonds and a major stock portfolio, the Fed would also run out of horsepower. At the first sign of economic weakness it would need a new trick to ease crisis conditions.

That's when administrative measures would be the next logical step for a central bank out of options.

Fifty years ago, nobody imagined the Fed would own $7 trillion worth of debt in an effort to fix interest rates at 0%. Five years ago, nobody imagined the Fed would buy junk bonds. Based on its actions, which grow progressively more extreme in each crisis, it will one day "bail in" the financial system taking idle bank deposits as hostages.

There's no limit to what central bankers will do to hold on to power. Creating trillions of dollars, choosing which companies get bail outs, mandatory bail-ins or preferential lifelines. It does all of this with the power to create limitless quantities of U.S. dollars.

The Fed creates its money in seconds, without providing notice to people using it to store their life savings. It can boost the supply of dollars with computer keystrokes. Gold on the other hand, requires effort to create. The gold supply grows at a naturally slow pace.

Gold, with a finite supply, is the ultimate protection against governments as they run out of radical new tricks to fix the crises they created.

Chapter 16 – Modern Monetary Theory (MMT)

Pay attention to the first thing that comes to mind about the man I'm about to describe.

He opens a trading account with £4,000 ($5,000). He asks his broker for the maximum margin loan possible. Think of this as a powerful yet dangerous line of credit.

Trading on margin magnifies gains on winning trades. As any experienced trader will tell you, it can also multiply losses. His broker agrees to extend him credit turning his £4,000 into £40,000. This allowed him to swing bigger than he could on his own.

Armed with £40,000 our trader steps into the market, carefully at first. After a few winners, confidence builds. No more fear.

Eight months later his initial £4,000 is worth £18,000. That's the net value of his account after factoring in all costs associated with his borrowing. He's up a remarkable 350%. Emboldened, he bets big on his next trade. It's a bust.

In one month, he turned a £14,000 profit into a £13,125 loss. Not only did he lose his initial £4,000, he owed his broker for losing borrowed funds. When asked about this later he said:

"The market can stay irrational longer than you can stay solvent."

He did eventually repay his brokerage debt. He also went on to become a famous author and economist.

The centerpiece of his fame was a theory that governments could use leverage (borrowing) to shorten recessions. They could borrow and spend heavily during periods of sluggish economic growth. This would boost the economy back to health.

As you can imagine, this was a popular message with politicians and bankers previously restricted by various gold standard-type limitations.

Our trader was John Maynard Keynes. He borrowed big and went bust. He made it all back later during a career of urging governments do the same.

When Debt Loses Its Power

Debt has a special power. There's a reason people call it "leverage."

Ancient Greek mathematician Archimedes said, *"Give me a place to stand and with a lever I will move the whole world."*

The concept is simple. Arrange the tools properly and you can move objects no group of people could budge even pushing with all their might.

Archimedes worked with the power of leverage to move heavy objects. Money leverage works in a similar way.

Say an apartment complex costs $2 million. You may be able to buy it with only $400,000 cash. You'd borrow the rest. That's leverage. With $400,000 invested, you now control a $2,000,000 asset.

All the way up the ladder leverage works the same way. That is, until it doesn't. Money leverage differs from what Archimedes discovered in one important way. The amount of leverage needed to move the same object grows exponentially when it comes to money.

When debt grows out of proportion to the system it levers, it loses its productivity. Simply put, the first dollar borrowed is the most powerful. Borrow more to pay back old loans and somewhere down the road you run into trouble.

To keep this up over time, larger piles of debt with cheaper borrowing rates are a must. Otherwise the debt comes due and it's unpayable.

While governments don't go bust in the same way as a company or a person, they can smother their economies.

Keynes Didn't Think This Out

Keynes died 26 years after his 1920 trading experience. His books, speeches, and ideas about government borrowing became gospel for academics. Those academics taught the Ph.D. students who'd go on to shape U.S. monetary policy.

The modern cycle of boom and bust in the U.S. started in the 1960s. With the dollar on a fixed exchange to gold beginning in 1944 it took a few years to get off track.

The U.S. slowly slipped into spendthrift behavior. Wars and welfare programs ramped up spending at home and abroad. Without cutbacks elsewhere, the U.S. ran persistent budget deficits. When tax revenues fell, it spent more citing the work of Keynes as a solution.

The past 20 years have seen this same pattern reach an extreme. Bubble, crisis, bubble, crisis with each bubble growing larger, and each crisis more traumatic. It can't go on this way forever.

Nature has a way of curing itself. You can't suppress forest fires indefinitely. If you do, the forest doesn't look natural. Fire has a way of eventually setting things straight.

The same goes for an economy dead set on preventing recession. The first few times seem to work. Managing things during the tough years becomes popular with politicians because it reduces economic hardship. Bankers love the extra scraps that fall when the government borrows big. Eventually bankers get tired of scraps and go for the whole steak.

The Final Boom

Each crisis calls for a more radical solution.

Economics is more like nature than economists would like to admit. Just as in nature, if you defy economic law you merely delay the inevitable. The more you delay nature, the more it pushes back. Eventually it's uncontrollable.

When it seems like the U.S. money system is out of options there's still one left.

Keynes touted government spending to soften a recession. Next came lowering borrowing costs to urge more lending and spending. Then it was big federal programs to take debt off the books of banks. This was followed by paying people not to work, negative interest rates which paradoxically charged bond buyers, and finally administrative measures forced buying of government debt. It seems like the end of the line, but it's not.

At this stage in the progression there'd be nobody willing to buy government debt, even if forced. Not even the speculators want to traffic in an endless flow of government junk.

Enter, Modern Monetary Theory (MMT). Here's how it works.

We know in normal times the U.S. government sells bonds to finance its spending deficit. That means spending in excess of what it receives in taxes.

Since nobody wants to buy its bonds anymore the Treasury sells one giant bond to the Federal Reserve. It carries a 0% interest rate, and it never matures. This is MMT.

Long ago when the Treasury sold tens of thousands of bonds to small investors it faced scrutiny. Lots of eyeballs watched over the government's finance decisions. With MMT, those days are over.

MMT is direct monetization of government expenditures. This means the jig is up. There's no need to talk down the deficit, promise restraint or even plan for that matter. Government decides what it wants to spend, and the Fed finances it.

Under MMT, the Treasury no longer has to hold a bond auction. Previously, it sold thousands of small bonds to investors, hedge funds, or companies. After all, for years U.S. debt was a triple-A-rated security. With its new financing scheme, that no longer matters.

If its annual budget shortfall is $3 trillion, the Treasury issues one bond to the Federal Reserve in exchange for $3 trillion newly created dollars. Again, this bond carries 0% interest and never matures. That means the Treasury will never repay or refinance this bond.

The premise of MMT is the government can create money to pay for anything from medical services to roads and bridges. It has the power to fund virtually limitless budget deficits by creating money to pay all bills in excess of tax revenue.

Your first reaction is likely, this must trigger major inflation. Afterall, a limitless supply of dollars certainly diminishes the value of dollars. Sort of. But, there's a bigger problem.

Inflation Is Not the Big Problem

To fully understand the role of inflation, let's do a quick review. The first dollar borrowed by a solvent government has immense power.

After the 1944 Bretton Woods agreement, the U.S. dollar had a tie to gold of 35:1. This exchange standard meant a foreign bank could present $35 and receive an ounce of U.S. gold.

If the U.S. government borrowed an extra $1, it was as good as gold.

When that extra dollar hit the economy, it boosted overall output. Let's say back then every $1 the Treasury borrowed and spent boosted U.S. GDP by $3. That means just a little borrowing went a long way during an economic soft patch.

This gets addictive. Soon you're solving every problem with more borrowed dollars.

Government debt is leverage. Keynes was right, it boosts economic activity. Over time, the power of that leverage wanes. Instead of every $1 borrowed producing $3 of additional GDP, it falls to $2, then $1. It finally falls to less than the amount borrowed making it a useless exercise.

Put in the terms of Archimedes, what once had the power to move the earth can barely move a pebble.

Those extra dollars end up in the U.S. money system. People save them up and use them as capital to buy assets. They borrow to boost the size of the assets they can buy. Money and credit expand.

That leads to more and more money chasing every imaginable opportunity looking for every cent of profitable gain. Eventually there's more money than opportunity.

Too Much Supply, Not Enough Demand

Next, all the surplus money starts chasing marginal opportunities. It builds more apartments than a city needs. It grows too much corn. It oversupplies the marketplace with more assets than the economy can handle.

This is a long-term consequence of using debt to fix every economic problem. It's a lot like building a tolerance to pain medication. When overused, debt loses its productivity.

Eventually the economy doesn't function. The natural processes that clear excess and rid the market of bad operators haven't functioned in decades.

Overbuilt and overburdened already, citizens of a once-free economic system cry out for help from the same people who caused the problem. MMT is their answer.

When You Hear the Messaging It's Already Too Late

When MMT kicks in it's too late. You can't buy fire insurance after your house burns down.

We haven't had a dollar to gold exchange for 50 years. That's part of the reason why gold is worth 4,400% more than it was when the U.S. ended that exchange. The supply of dollars grew much faster than the supply of gold.

Remember, U.S. citizens could legally own gold again beginning in 1974. It surged in value through the end of the decade but paused for the following two. The 1980s and 1990s were a period of controlled money policy.

Interest rates fell consistently over that period. Falling rates means lower borrowing costs. When this process happens in a steady way it creates a reliable climate for investing in paper assets.

Paper assets mean the value of something on paper. The company with billions of dollars in debt is worth a lot as long as it maintains access to more debt at lower cost. Once that access ends, the company returns to its true value.

Hard assets are the opposite of paper assets. Their value isn't tied to the paper money and credit system. Hard assets hurt if you drop them on your foot. Paper assets don't.

After its break from gold in 1971 the U.S. forced trading partners to use the dollar. That means it maintained its position as the world's formidable currency even after abandoning any tie to gold. It did not hold up however as a store of value, failing to meet one of the key definitions of money.

The money games of the last 20 years set us up for the extreme bubble to crisis pattern we can't escape today. While there are a few tricks left to play on dollar holders, there aren't many.

MMT will pull the U.S. from its most severe crisis. That's why if you pay attention, you'll see articles touting MMT today, well in advance of that final crisis.

This is how media messaging works. Float the idea, let people say it's crazy. After a pause, float it again and it sounds less crazy. Finally, during the next major crisis deliver the formerly radical but now familiar idea as a bold solution to societal woes.

When you see MMT in action, watch out. It means outright financing of government deficits with no intent to repay. It's direct monetization of government spending. What comes after the crisis that causes won't be pretty.

Government's don't let go of power gracefully. Look across history. They hold the grip until there's nothing left. U.S. economic supremacy is all its current leaders have ever known. Their natural instinct won't be to let go. It will be to grip harder.

They've already got the technology to do it. Created by intelligence, perfected by an unknowing private marketplace, it's set to turn the U.S. and the world into a financial prison.

Chapter 17 – FedCoin

Total control. It's the ultimate desire of any government. When the U.S. runs into a crisis that's too big to fix, it will be a necessity.

That day is not far off. In fact, technology already exists that could be used to make it happen. It would give government complete control of every dollar ever created. It would know when, where, how, and why every dollar changed hands.

This is much more than digital money. It's instant access to every financial asset you own.

This technology is impervious to computer hackers. Counterfeiting, tax evasion, and financial transgressions of any type are impossible.

Sound like science fiction? It's already in use in the private markets today.

Lenin said, "The capitalists will sell us the rope with which we will hang them."

It's possible that far in advance of implementing this technology, the intelligence community planted its seed in the private markets. It assumed, correctly, that private speculators would compete to perfect it.

Once perfected, no more need for the speculators. Government's perfect tool for total money control would already be in place.

Does This Sound Normal?

See if you think something sounds a little off about this story.

In August 2008 an anonymous web user registers the domain name bitcoin.org. Two months later a post appears. It's a white paper entitled, *Bitcoin: A Peer-to-Peer Electronic Cash System.*

The paper's author is Satoshi Nakamoto. No one knows who Satoshi is.

His paper is brilliant. It explains that the traditional financial system relies on intermediaries to process payments. Whether it's a bank, title company, or credit card issuer, every payment sent from one person to another passes through a third party.

Long ago, this made sense. Banks and other third parties created trust between two people who didn't know each other otherwise. For a small fee, the bank provided neutral ground.

Satoshi said the advent of the internet age reduced the usefulness of these third parties. They were a burden. In the 2008 crisis they caused financial distrust instead of solving it. Curiously, he posted the paper at the very beginning of the crisis, so he either wrote quickly or had incredible instincts.

In light of this old cumbersome system that failed us, Satoshi outlined a means of transacting between individuals without using a third party. Instead of leaning on those third parties for trust, his system used math.

Better still, instead of relying on a central authority to issue his proposed digital currency, users of the currency create it by performing calculations on an open network. The coins were rewards. He called them Bitcoins.

Bitcoins are rewarded to users whose computers connect to the network to help solve cryptographic math problems that become progressively more difficult. That means it takes more and more computing power over time making rewards more valuable. There would be a finite limit of Bitcoins available as a reward, 21 million to be exact.

While you're welcome to read the entire nine-page white paper online at bitcoin.org, the basic premise is simple.

Initially, the value of a Bitcoin was less than $1. I know because I had a meeting with a social acquaintance in 2009 who suggested we use old computers to "mine" these coins. This means we string these old computers together to run the code-crunching protocol and take coins as rewards.

This guy was a major cheapskate. He was however tech-savvy. He had a business selling spare electronic parts. He obsessed over extracting every cent of value from anything resalable. While worth at least $1 million at the time, this guy was so cheap he lived in a duplex operating the business out of the other side.

I told him it sounded like a dumb idea. At the time I wanted to buy single family homes, gold, and gold stocks. I wasn't interested in much else.

Turns out, my acquaintance had the better idea. My guess is we could have mined at least 1,000 Bitcoin with his plan. Remember, in the old days it didn't take much computing power. As the next chart illustrates, 1,000 Bitcoin hit a peak value of $18.5 million eight years later.

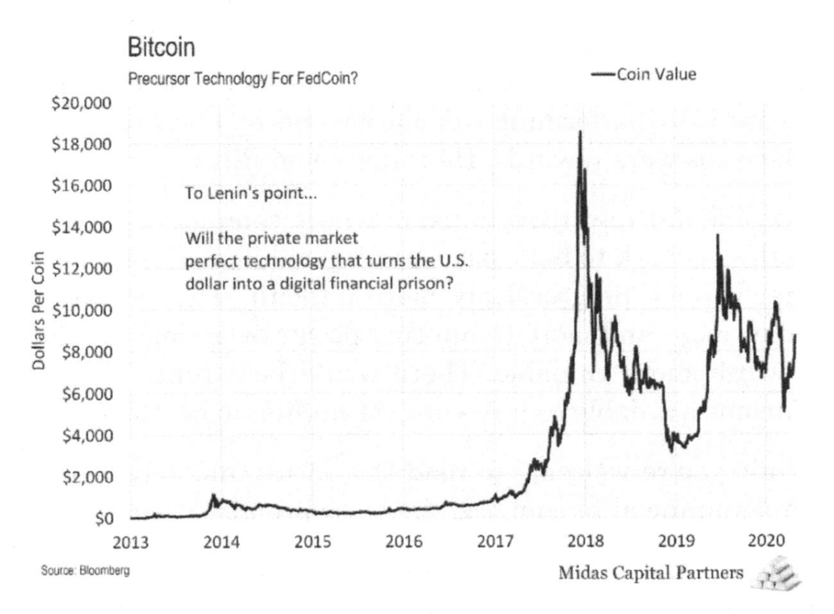

Bitcoin mania took hold. I heard about the idea endlessly from friends in the early days. Keep in mind, I wrote a rogue finance blog, I visited conferences with like-minded types, and I rarely turned down the chance to go see or do something that sounded interesting.

All the while, I was a gold investor. I understood the history of gold and its usefulness in times of monetary turbulence. I also understood the gold market, which we'll get into in Part III.

Look Past the Speculative Frenzy

In August of 2017, in the middle of the Bitcoin speculation frenzy, I went to a party in Vancouver, British Columbia. I met a 28-year old billionaire with his entire net worth held in Bitcoin.

At dinner I asked him if he was open to any financial advice. I advised he sell half the bitcoin and buy a collection of apartments, farms, billboards, warehouses and about anything he could find that spread his wealth beyond Bitcoin. Keep in mind, just half. I said he could leave the rest in Bitcoin.

He said absolutely not. When I asked why he said, *"We're going to change the world."*

Maybe he will. But I'm betting on the bad guys when it comes to controlling the money supply.

Governments have the right to create currency. They mandate its use either by law or by gun. I've never known them to allow competition.

What interested me from day one with Bitcoin was the architecture behind it. Satoshi's idea could become a mathematical framework for distributing payments of all types.

He called the technology "blockchain." He referred to the blocks as equations solved that generated a coin as reward. These blocks, once solved, formed a brick trail of sorts documenting each transaction.

There was no need for a central overseer as long as there were a sufficient number of computers hooked to the network. This "distributed" the power to control his digital currency across many users - the exact opposite of a central authority.

When someone wanted to sell a Bitcoin, the process made a lot of sense. There were two things required for a valid transaction. He called these "keys." One was public, one was private.

This works a lot like opening your safety deposit box at the local bank. The banker has one master key that opens every box. You have a private key that only fits your box. However, no box will open without both keys turning at the same time.

A Bitcoin transaction needed the seller's private encryption key as well as the public encryption key which other users could see.

From the early days this seemed like an obvious way to upend the traditional financial system. For instance, title companies make a fortune processing real estate transactions. The whole concept of title insurance is useless with blockchain technology. The house can't change hands until all outstanding liabilities clear. All users on the network can see and verify that.

The same goes for recording stock ownership, issuing dividends, and tracking other financial ownership. Blockchain can radically reduce the cost of administering these processes. Without the need for a financial intermediary, users deal directly with each other.

What I did not expect was the speculative frenzy that came along with Bitcoin's price surge.

Bitcoin was the original digital payment token, or "cryptocurrency." Once it took off speculators started creating similar coins hoping to stake their digital fortune.

As of Spring 2020 there were 5,392 digital currencies according to Yahoo Finance. PizzaCoin claims to change the way you order pizza. CasinoCoin facilitates gambling, and so on.

This is what a mania looks like. When anything runs from $1 to $18,000 every thinking capitalist jumps in to get a piece of it. Most of these knockoff coins will end up worthless.

Interestingly, while this frenzy minted billionaires, the government sat back and let it happen. I'm not suggesting government has a role in everything, don't get me wrong. But we're talking about what Bitcoin faithful publicly called a "money revolution."

It's Already in the Works

Something doesn't seem right about Satoshi's story.

At Bitcoin's peak value the alleged creator's net worth was more than $19 billion. Nobody knows who he is, where he is, or what he did with his Bitcoin fortune. His hoard of coins appears untouched. While it's possible Satoshi lives a quiet life with no possessions, it's unlikely.

Computer scientists went back over his activity on the Bitcoin network. They compiled all of the timestamps left behind on each of his posts. He almost never accessed the network between the hours of 12:00 AM and 6:00 AM Eastern Time.

There were about 500 of these timestamps to analyze. They started in late 2008 and stopped in 2010.

Satoshi Nakamoto appears to be a Japanese name. His white paper reads like plain American English. Some of his online comments between inception and 2010 use slang phrases common to British English.

Regardless, the elusive Satoshi anonymously fired the starting gun that set a stampede of speculators in motion. The result more than a decade later is a practical, useful and efficient digital currency.

Consider the possibility that a shadowy branch of government let the private marketplace perfect a digital currency that will in the end give it total control.

Ultimate Control

I received this email from a friend who asked I redact his name and the country mentioned.

"...I met a guy who is head of the Central Bank of [redacted]'s 'crypto project'... the guy is a decorated special forces soldier with a military intelligence background and an economics degree... He told me... "we love crypto, governments love crypto... we will eventually finalize our project, which will be for a crypto [redacted] national currency. We will probably let it be produced through a bitcoin style mining solution but we will set the difficulty of the solution so that we can control the money supply.

The crypto [redacted] will report every single transaction to the tax office as well... once we get it done, we will ban physical currency and then ban all competitors... we will know if you buy competitors because the crypto [redacted] will flag such transactions to us...."

Think about this for a minute. "We love crypto" means the intelligence community sees tremendous value in the same features Bitcoin proponents love.

The difference between Bitcoin and what this guy discusses is extremely important to understand.

Bitcoin eliminated the central authority by creating a peer-controlled computing network. Essentially, transactions, or "blocks," build on to a chain. This "blockchain" is the real power of Bitcoin. The coin value is separate and secondary.

However, a blockchain can utilize the same cryptographic technology while having a central authority. This is what the former special forces soldier says they'll do.

What this means is private market speculators took Bitcoin and ran with it. They developed immense knowhow in computing related to the Bitcoin concept. At the same time, computing power continued to multiply.

My friend's contact says governments think this is fantastic. That means it's on the way.

While people flock to ATMs and hoard cash now, governments could outlaw that overnight.

During the 2020 virus scare media outlets reported on the dangers of handling cash. They alleged the virus could live on paper currency for long periods.

Governments hate cash because it's anonymous. They've done everything possible to limit it. Try paying for any serious purchase in cash and watch the store clerk tremble while calling the manager for help. You're assumed to be a criminal for carrying more than $20 these days.

In addition to being increasingly difficult to use, cash is on the way out. As that day approaches, look for stories of how a digital dollar would be good for everyone. Expect to hear media praise, positive study results touting its effectiveness, all the while maligning cash as a dangerous relic of a bygone era. FedCoin will be the solution to all those problems.

But there's still time. Cash today is a last vestige of what will later look like incredible freedom.

You can buy untraceable, impossible-to-destroy physical gold with cash today. But if the government flipped the switch on FedCoin, it will know everywhere you bought every ounce of gold, what you paid for it, and where you put it after driving home from the gold dealer.

The window to protect wealth with gold is still open today. Now let's look at the best ways to do it, and more importantly, the ones to avoid.

Part III – Your Ultimate Gold Handbook

Introduction – Let's Get Positioned

Now is the time to take action.

We learned about gold's history as sound money. Governments, kings, and the world's wealthiest families trust it as a reliable store of value.

Gold doesn't depend on anyone or anything for its value. The value of a building depends on tenants paying rent. The value of a bond depends on reliable interest payments. Stocks depend on company profits. Gold depends on nothing. In a time where other assets fail, gold shines.

We also know gold is scarce, with its supply growing at only 1.5% per year. The growth rate of money and credit has no physical limit.

If you formed a perfect square cube using all the gold ever mined in human history, it would fit inside the infield of a baseball diamond. That cube is worth roughly $10 trillion today. While that sounds like a lot, it's a fraction of the world's debt pile barreling towards $300 trillion.

$10 trillion worth of gold against $300 trillion worth of debt means every $1 of gold holds up $30 of debt. Meanwhile, the world debt pile grows faster than the world economy. Some debts will go bad. Gold won't.

1980-2000 was a good time for debt. Interest rates fell precipitously. Bondholders looked smart. Meanwhile, gold sat idle. Then came the debt binge.

Today, swimming in debt, the countries, companies, and individuals of the world have all they can handle. The odds of repayment are low. Worse, they pay next to nothing to borrow.

This destroys the age-old argument against gold, it doesn't pay interest, and it costs money to safely store.

In 2019, a record $17 trillion worth of world debt carried negative interest rates. That means savers paid money to own bonds. Bonds carry risk of default. Gold does not.

The stage looks set for gold to become the world's most sought-after asset. With little attention from mainstream finance, getting into gold might be confusing. We'll clear that up.

From coins to bars, exchange-traded funds (ETFs), mining stocks, and the world's most profitable business, gold royalty companies, we'll cover it all.

Since nothing in this world is permanent, we'll even talk about when to sell gold. There will be a time when other assets present a better opportunity. We're a long way from that today. So, let's get started.

Chapter 18 – How Much Gold Is Enough?

Before rushing out to buy gold it's important to determine how much you want to own. The best way to do this is by looking at what percentage of your assets you want in gold.

It seems like everyone wants to make money investing. They're always looking for a tip or some edge on the market. But that's not how the pros do it. They look at the whole pie and decide how big each slice should be.

You can do the same thing. In a matter of minutes, with a Microsoft Excel table an eighth grader could handle, you can see your whole pie.

People say they don't have time for this. They want to preserve hard-earned wealth. They also want to make a little more of it. But they don't have time to plan.

No business can achieve success without a plan. The same goes for individuals.

It's impossible to plan without looking at what you have first. If you haven't done this, do it today. If you have, update it with current prices and values.

Real estate, stocks, retirement accounts, cash, life insurance and all other assets combined give you the total pie. Once you see it on paper you can determine what kind of slice gold gets.

It's a mistake to buy as much gold as you can afford, or an amount that feels like a lot. Good stewards of wealth put a percentage on it. Look at the total pie and decide what percentage goes to gold.

As Little as 3%

Think about this. If every professionally managed investment account in the world put just 3% of its assets into gold, the price would go through the roof. There is just not enough gold to meet that demand.

That's 3%. If gold goes on a run, some people would shoot for much more.

As of 2017, there were $79.2 trillion of assets under management in the world according to the research firm Statista. That number counts assets managed by someone charging a fee. There's no way 3% of those assets could go to gold.

With a total value of $10 trillion in early 2020, gold is a tight market. Making things worse, jewelry, government vaults, and private hoards eat up most of that gold. By my count, there's about $1.5-2 trillion worth of physical gold available for investment.

Most asset managers hold zero gold. Most individuals hold zero gold. The last time gold had a mainstream following was the late 1970s. That means a 60-year old asset manager spent his entire career ignoring gold. That's about to change.

Part of what prompted me to write this book in the spring of 2020 was a comment from my Zen teacher. Knowing my background, we often talk about investing. Pursuit of Zen doesn't have to happen in poverty.

He asked his wealth advisor to buy him some gold. The response was, "I will lose my license if I do that." Not only is that not true, it's hard to imagine a professional thinking it's possible.

You can buy physical gold on the New York Stock Exchange (NYSE) with the click of a button. As we'll discuss later, there's more than one fund trading on the stock exchange that holds gold bullion in a vault for a small fee.

How could a money manager "lose his license" buying an NYSE-listed fund? The better question is, do you think these "wealth managers" have enough foresight to get you involved in gold before it moves higher?

It's unlikely you'll find gold in any of the recommended investment formulas followed by wealth managers today. Ask yours about it and see what kind of reaction you get.

Meanwhile, adding just a small percentage of gold to an investment portfolio produces more stable returns. The World Gold Council studies the effect of adding gold to portfolios. It publishes a free report called The Relevance of Gold as A Strategic Asset. You can access it free of charge at gold.org.

In the 2019 edition of the report, the Council calculated the effect of adding 2%, 5% or 10% gold to the average pension fund portfolio. They cite data showing how holding gold would have increased returns and lowered market risk.

Even with that knowledge, most professional managers don't want to own gold today. That will change in a gold bull market. By the end, when gold sells for much higher prices, they'll insist you get some before it's too late.

Today, it's early. You might have to make the decision on your own.

Consider what 3% of assets might look like. With a $1 million net worth, it's $30,000 allocated to gold. With $100,000 net worth, it's $3,000. With $10,000 it's $300.

The right amount varies by person. I know people with 20% of their assets in gold and gold stocks. Everyone is different.

The dollar amount matters less than getting the percentage right. The best money managers focus on the percentage allocated to each asset. You can do it too. The next time you meet with your wealth advisor you'll be armed with the facts.

Once you decide how much gold is right for you, it's time to look at how to own it.

Chapter 19 – Gold Bars

Physical gold is the starting point of any gold portfolio.

I co-managed a gold stock fund a decade ago. That means we bought and sold gold stocks every day. We'll get into some of those experiences later.

When we met with clients, they almost always asked for advice on how to structure their gold holdings. We always told them physical comes first. That means, your physical gold is the bedrock of your gold holdings. If you ask me, it's the bedrock of your wealth too.

Gold is wealth insurance. In my mind, it's not something that shoots higher in value creating vast new wealth. More likely, gold protects against a big erosion of wealth.

As far as tremendous investment gains from gold, those usually come from holding stock in the right mining or royalty company. I've been a part of several massive gains. That often happens overnight as the result of discovering a big new gold deposit. But that's not wealth insurance, that's speculating.

You wouldn't gamble with a fire insurance policy on your home. You also hope you don't need to use it. That's the way to see physical gold. Over the years I've learned many wealthy families see it the same way.

Pure, "hold in your hand gold" is unlike any other asset. If you've never touched a piece of gold, try it. Jewelry doesn't count. It's often a gold alloy. That means it's mixed with cheaper metals to strengthen the gold, which on its own shows dents and dings too easily.

You know the purity of gold by its karat rating. By law, gold advertised for sale in the U.S. must display a karat rating.

24-karat gold is pure. You'll rarely see 24-karat gold jewelry. 12-karat gold means 50% gold 50% alloy. While less valuable, a 12-karat gold bracelet would be much more durable than one that's 24-karat.

The karat system started out as a weighting system used by Mediterranean traders. Passing through town they'd trade a piece of gold or other precious metal for supplies. Since trust between strangers was a problem, they turned to nature for an honest solution.

The region is home to the carob tree, which produces a pod filled with carob seeds. Strangely, each carob seed weighs almost precisely the same amount. With a balance scale, traders felt comfortable verifying weights of precious items using one, two or three or any number of carob seeds. Carob became carat, then karat, and lives on today as the required rating for all advertised jewelry.

We're interested in pure gold. That means jewelry isn't the best way to store wealth in gold. Family heirlooms, rings, watches and other gold accessories are valuable. But for storing serious wealth in gold we need something more practical.

Gold Bars

Remember the gold bars in the 1964 James Bond classic *Goldfinger*? Those were fake. However, they were accurately sized and colored to resemble real gold bars.

The bars pictured in the movie were meant to be 400 ounces of pure gold. The industry calls them "good delivery bars." It means they meet the delivery standards required by the London Bullion Market Association (LBMA). Refiners pour gold bars accordingly before sending them to LBMA vaults.

The bars are not very big. I've seen several in person. They average about 10"x3" but it's the purity that counts. The LBMA requires 995 parts per thousand gold. That means 99.5% purity.

When it comes to gold ounces, don't confuse them with traditional ounces. That means an ounce of gold and an ounce of beef are not the same thing.

Gold trades in troy ounces. A troy ounce is roughly 10% heavier than a standard ounce.

The origin of the troy ounce is said to be the trading post of Troye, France, around the 15th century. Troy ounces measured grains which had ties to English silver coins around that era. Regardless, we use troy ounces for gold. Missing that detail could leave you on the wrong end of a physical gold transaction.

Those 400-ounce gold bars are the largest common denomination. They're also very heavy weighing in at 27.43 pounds each. Gold is one of the densest metals on earth. It weighs more than 19-times as much as water. Don't let the small size of these 400-ounce bars fool you.

I mentioned touring the New York Federal Reserve about twenty years ago. On the tour we took an elevator way down to the gold vault. I don't think they allow it these days.

I'll never forget the men in the vault wore aluminum shoes. The tour guide said accidently dropping a gold bar could fracture your foot. The rounded aluminum shoe was a safety measure.

The Fed vault, like most gold vaults, sees gold moved from stall to stall over and over again. The gold belongs to countries, companies or trading houses. Moving it to another stall means a transfer of ownership to settle some balance of payments.

At first it seems interesting, but eventually moving gold bars with a forklift from one stall to another would get old. However, that gold anchors some nation or major entity in a massive financial transaction. It's the bedrock of national wealth, surely it should be the bedrock of ours too.

Gold bars aren't for everyone. They make the most sense when buying gold means moving serious wealth. Common sizes of gold bars are:

- 400 ounce
- 100 ounce
- 1 kilogram (32.1507 ounce)
- 10 ounce
- 1 ounce
- 10 gram
- 1 gram

400-ounce gold bars are the top of the food chain. One of those good delivery bars shown in the Bond film will set you back $690,000 assuming gold trades for $1,725/oz. Most individuals won't start there.

Even for the extremely wealthy, these bars aren't always practical. You might want to sell 100 or 200 ounces of gold one day and storing wealth in all 400-ounce bars makes that difficult.

While the 400-ounce bar meets the LBMA delivery standards, the American equivalent COMEX in New York accepts 100-ounce bars. A 100-ounce gold bar runs $172,500 assuming the same gold price.

Meeting COMEX standards means the exchange accepts this bar from customers for settlement of trades. You likely won't use that feature, but it's how the refiner pours the bar. Think of it as a standard set by the exchange to reduce re-inspection and confusion between trading parties.

After 100-ounce bars come 1 kilogram. This is where average investors may start to get involved. I've suggested these to several wealthy friends looking for a way to get started. They don't take up much space. They're about the size of a Hershey candy bar, only much heavier.

10-ounce bars are even more in reach at $17,250. However, this is where some caution comes into play. A decade ago, there were incidents of fraud where scammers used cheaper tungsten metal for the core of 10-ounce bars. This is a huge problem. People only discovered the fraud by X-raying the bars.

Using a reputable refiner and a reputable dealer eliminates much of this risk. While a fake is certainly possible, it's less likely if you take basic precautions.

There will usually be a small certificate of authenticity matching a number imprinted on the bar. PAMP is a well-known refiner in Switzerland. Johnson Matthey is another with facilities in the U.S. There are others.

Buying gold in bar form is often the cheapest way to do it. With any gold transaction there will be some difference between the actual price of gold and the price the broker quotes you. This is the spread or broker's commission.

Say gold trades for $1,725/oz. That's known as the "spot" price. You might do the math and find there's a 1% or 2% difference between the broker's sale price and the spot price you see quoted in the market.

The small percentage difference between those two numbers is the spread. You'll see it when buying and selling. When it comes to gold bars, shop around to find the lowest spread. Also, be sure to check the market for the most accurate price just before you buy.

However, don't compromise on quality. If someone offers you gold below the spot price, that's a red flag. Odds are it's either fake or stolen. Look for an imprint stamp on the top of the bar identifying the refinery that produced it. You should only buy gold bars produced at a reputable refinery.

If you want to buy gold bars know what size suits you. Then be sure to check the spot price. That will help you calculate the spread being charged by the broker. Let the broker make some money, just not too much.

The gold market trades 23-½ hours a day Sunday evening through Friday afternoon. You can almost always get an accurate price quote. That means you can order a gold bar almost anytime.

Don't Mess with Grams

There are smaller denominations of gold bars. The smallest is 1 gram which is about $55 worth of gold assuming a spot price of $1,725/oz. Remember, you'll also pay a premium to the dealer.

Small gold bars are not worth the effort in many cases. One gram of gold doesn't look like much. There may be better ways to get started if you're working with a small amount of money.

If you're starting out, 1-ounce coins might be the place to begin. That said, you'll need to know what to buy and where to find them. Not all 1-ounce coins are the same.

Chapter 20 – Common Gold Coins

For the average investor, 1-ounce gold coins are a great starting point.

Most coins come in half-ounce or even quarter-ounce denominations. Stick with the 1-ounce version. It's easy to value if you go to sell the coin. Fractional ounces trade with a spread just like other gold ounces. Since the value of a fractional ounce is lower, the spread might eat up a bigger percentage of the transaction. It's just not worth it.

Gold is not just wealth insurance, it's also wealth storage. Ten ounces of gold coins won't take up much space. Worth over $17,250 at current prices, this stack of ten coins is barely over one inch tall.

10 1 oz gold coins

Many countries mint 1-ounce coins. The Romans minted coins, modern countries mint coins, even out of the way places like Ukraine mint beautiful gold coins. While all of these coins are worth seeing, only a few of them are worth owning.

If you want to keep things easy, stick with these 1-ounce gold coins:

- South African Krugerrand
- Canadian Maple Leaf
- American Eagle

All three of these coins are easy to trade. Walk into a coin or jewelry store almost anywhere on planet earth and the dealer will instantly know what to offer you for one of these. That means you've got headache-free "hold in your hand" gold.

South African Krugerrand

South Africa mints the Krugerrand. In the early 1980's it's said the Krugerrand made up around 90% of all gold coins circulating.

The country uses the rand as its currency. The Kruger part comes from Paul Kruger who led the country as President in the late 19th century. His picture is on the front of the coin.

Back of a 1 oz gold Krugerrand

South Africa is a major gold producer. It started minting the Krugerrand in 1967. During the 1970's gold boom these coins were popular and easy to trade. There are around 50 million of them in existence today.

In addition to being common, the Krugerrand is durable. At 22-karats, the coin is a copper-gold alloy. Adding copper makes the coin resistant to scratches and dings. It also makes it heavier.

The 1-ounce gold Krugerrand actually weighs 1.09 troy ounces. Don't think you're getting extra gold, it's the copper alloy that increases the weight.

Canadian Maple Leaf

The Canadian Maple Leaf is the purest gold coin. It carries 0.9999 fineness. Canadians call this "4 nines." It means the coin is 99.99% pure gold, which is noted on the front.

1 oz gold Maple Leaf

Where the Krugerrand is durable, the Maple Leaf is not. While beautiful, the coin dings and dents easily. If you buy Maples, be careful storing them. Even banging into one another can leave a mark. Dealers might give you a hard time when you go to sell one with a dent or ding.

Canada is a major gold producer. It's part of the culture. Consequently, gold is easy to buy. Many currency exchange stores in Canada offer gold by the ounce. This is less common in the U.S. and other parts of the world.

They're also proud of the "4 nines." I visited an office in Toronto in 2016 and found this coin on display, heavily secured of course. At 100 kilograms (3,215 ounces) of solid gold the coin is worth about $5.5 million as of mid-2020 with gold trading at just over $1,700/oz.

3,215 oz Canadian Maple Leaf at a solid .9999 fine gold

The Maple Leaf is a good coin choice for individual investors. It looks like what you'd expect from gold: bright, brilliant and delicate. If you store it next to more durable coins, be sure to protect it.

American Eagle

When we say American Eagle, we're talking about 1-ounce gold coins produced after 1986.

Remember, in 1933 Roosevelt made owning gold a felony. He commanded citizens to turn in coins, melting them down to form bars which the U.S. later squandered. That said, there are some pre-1933 gold coins called American Eagles.

We'll talk about older coins in the next chapter. For now, we're interested in common coins. These common coins carry the value of 1 troy ounce of gold. They're easy to trade. Eagles are some of the easiest for Americans.

The front of the coin shows Lady Liberty. This was the same with older versions of the coin. The back features a soaring eagle.

American Eagle whose front side features Lady Liberty

The American Eagle is 22-karat gold just like the Krugerrand. The U.S. government guarantees the fineness and quality of the gold Eagle. It also mandates that the U.S. Mint source gold from U.S. production.

The 22-karat Krugerrand is a copper-gold alloy giving it a slightly reddish hue. The Eagle is copper-silver-gold. Both coins weight 1.09 troy ounces.

The Eagle is a highly respected coin. Dealers trust its purity and consistency. The U.S. mints between 500,000-1,000,000 annually. Production varies by year.

When buying any of these common coins, be wary of mint sets and collector's editions. There's nothing wrong with the gold in these coins. It's the additional charges you can avoid.

For instance, the U.S. Mint will change the Eagle in the coming years. It's an anti-counterfeit design change. If the Mint offered special commemorative edition Eagles for an additional fee, it's not worth it for our purpose.

Remember, this is about wealth storage. We want gold that's easy to buy, reliable, and easy to sell. One-ounce gold coins from the U.S., Canada and South Africa are the best for that purpose.

There Are Others

If you can't help yourself, there are other 1-ounce coins from countries all around the world.

The 1-ounce Chinese Panda picked up steam a few years ago. There's a 1-ounce Koala from Australia. I personally like the 1-ounce Austrian Philharmonic, which pays tribute to the Vienna Philharmonic Orchestra. It's about 15% larger than other coins with similar gold content. I find the detail of the coin amazing.

Mexico produced interesting gold coins for many years. The country is a big gold producer and the largest silver producer in the world. Its 50-peso gold coin weighs 37.5 grams, or about 1.21 ounces. If you have one and go to sell it, don't forget about that extra 0.21 ounce.

50-peso Mexican gold coin

At the end of the day, the average gold investor may be best served sticking with common coins. Buying and storing 1-100 of these common gold coins is easy. That means storing $1,750-$175,000 in a small space, or several small spaces.

Most importantly, selling coins is easy. One at a time or all at once, you shouldn't run into any trouble with these easy to recognize 1-ounce common coins.

If you don't have a trusted source for coins, try one of these three companies. I know the principals of each firm. Any one of them will be a good starting point.

- Fisher Precious Metals +1.800.390.8576 – fisherpreciousmetals.com
- Schiff Gold +1.888-GOLD-160 – schiffgold.com
- Gainesville Coins +1.813.482.9300 – gainesvillecoins.com

Don't be afraid to compare prices, shipping and customer experiences. In the end, it's important to feel good about the broker you do business with. You might end up doing more business with them than you anticipated. That's when a trusted relationship becomes very important.

Over time, you might find other coins interesting. If that happens, you're now a coin collector. And that's a whole different ballgame.

Chapter 21 – Collectible Gold Coins

In 2002, Sotheby's sold a gold coin weighing just over 1 troy ounce for $7.59 million. At the time, it was the highest price paid for any U.S. gold coin.

The coin was a gold 1933 Saint-Gaudens Double Eagle. To my knowledge, it's the rarest gold coin in the world.

Outside of the one auctioned at Sotheby's in 2002, an estimated 13 others exist around the world today. Two of those are in the U.S. government's national coin collection held at the Smithsonian. However, no one knows for sure exactly how many 1933 Double Eagles exist or where the others are.

I once met a coin expert who claimed he had seen several of the illicit, missing coins with his own eyes. He wouldn't go into more detail. In fact, he didn't even want to talk about it.

The 1933 Saint-Gaudens Double Eagle is a dangerous coin. It's dangerous to own that is. If you have one, don't tell anybody. Possessing the coin could land you in a U.S. federal prison.

The U.S. produced gold Saint-Gaudens Double Eagles from 1907-1933. The coin weighs just over one ounce yet contains only 0.9675 ounces of gold. The balance is copper alloy for strength and durability.

Sculptor Augustus Saint-Gaudens designed the coin. Coin collectors call them “Saints” for short. In total, around 70 million of the coins came out of the U.S. Mint system.

In early 1933 the U.S. Mint began striking that year’s Saint. Starting on March 6 it struck 445,500 1-ounce gold Saints before abruptly stopping on April 5.

If you recall, that’s right at the time Roosevelt’s executive order barred U.S. citizens from owning physical gold. The order allowed certain collectible coins in limited quantities. However, Roosevelt ordered the recently minted 1933 Saints destroyed.

Here’s where things get a little gray. I’ll tell you what I’ve learned over the years as a coin collector. However, it’s impossible to validate my take on this because no one knows exactly what happened inside the Philadelphia branch of the U.S. Mint in April 1933.

The 1933 Saint never entered circulation. That means it never became official U.S. currency like prior year Saints going back to 1907.

Each gold Saint minted between 1907-1933 states “Twenty Dollars” on the rear of the coin. Until Roosevelt confiscated gold held by citizens, the official gold price was $20.67/oz. Each Saint contained 0.9675 troy ounces of gold valued at $20 even.

The real intention of FDR’s executive order was to raise the official price of gold to $35/oz after confiscating it. There was no point in letting the 1933 Saints leave the mint.

Only a select few Mint employees had access to the 1933 Saints in the short time they existed. Prior to melting the coins it's my guess one of those employees took around 20 of them, maybe more, leaving an equal number of older Saints in their place.

It's easy to see why an employee wouldn't consider this theft. Ounce for ounce, there was no gold missing. The Mint's detailed accounting kept track of the gold. Since there was no change in gold content, they wouldn't notice a thing. This made the missing coins look like a harmless souvenir.

Nine of those estimated 20 missing 1933 Saints surfaced in the years that followed. U.S. Treasury officials turned the missing coins into an all-out manhunt. They documented and destroyed the nine coins. This left only 11 after accounting for the two held at the Smithsonian.

King Farouk of Egypt had one of them. The U.S. Treasury went to the full extent of diplomatic limits trying to get it back. When Farouk lost power in a 1952 coup his coin disappeared. He had an estimated 8,500 collectible coins, but his 1933 Saint was surely the most valuable.

If you somehow find yourself in possession of a 1933 Saint, you might want to keep it to yourself. While the coin has inestimable value, it's illicit.

However, millions of 1-ounce gold Saints minted between 1907-1932 exist today. It's one of the most popular collectible coins out there. Saints are fun to own, if you know what you're doing.

Stay Away from Collectible Coins

For most people, collectible coins are a no-fly zone.

We're interested in gold as wealth insurance. Collectible gold coins still contain gold value. The difference is buyers pay an additional premium for rarity. This varies widely and can get novices in a lot of trouble.

I've heard horror stories. People call up a marginal coin dealer looking for a 1-ounce gold Krugerrand. They hang up the phone after paying five-times the price of gold for an allegedly rare coin the salesman said would appreciate in value.

That's why you should generally stay away from the collectible coin market. It's a racket. Stick to the common 1-ounce coins we discussed in Chapter 20. More importantly, stick with reputable dealers who won't use those common coins as bait to then sell you more expensive collectible coins.

That said, if you turn coin collecting into a hobby, it can be lucrative. I've had a lot of fun with collectible coins for close to 20 years. The trick is to focus on one or two specific types of coins. This way you're expert enough to know what a good deal is.

Take the pre-1933 gold Saint-Gaudens for example. There are millions of them available that legally avoided Roosevelt's confiscation order. Coins with dates from 1907-1932 have wildly varied values. That turns collecting them into a treasure hunt.

The 1924 gold Saint-Gaudens Double Eagle pictured is worth roughly the value of its gold content. Today, that's about $1,660. Remember, the Saint contains 0.9675 troy ounces of gold with the balance copper.

This coin might fetch a small premium today with physical gold in high demand. However, there is no collectible value because someone "cleaned" the coin.

1924 "cleaned" coin has no collectible value

The rating agency identified this coin as cleaned. The details noted on the top of the case point that out.

The coin is still gold, which certainly has value. It's also authentic. At nearly 100-years old there is some value there. However, as a collectible it has no value because someone tried to polish the coin with a mild abrasive.

If you paid a premium for this coin you'd be out of luck. That means with its gold content worth $1,660, if someone sold it to you for $2,000, they scammed you.

Remember, there are two value components to collectible coins. One is the gold in the coin. The second is collectible value, the premium assigned to rarity and condition of an older coin. When someone cleaned this coin, they destroyed that extra boost to value.

It's hard to recognize a coin as cleaned. Compared to most people, I know a lot about gold Saints. This one got past me. I did not notice the cleaning, even after inspecting the coin with a jeweler's loop. A coin dealer friend also didn't notice. The rating agency, Professional Coin Grading Service (PCGS), did notice.

PCGS is the leading coin rating service, but there are many others. Serious coin collectors trust PCGS and its chief competitor Numismatic Guaranty Corporation (NGC) more than those others. That means when one of these top rating agencies assigns a value, it tends to hold during a sales process. Lesser agencies don't carry the same power.

While the last coin had just under 1-ounce of gold value and $0 of collectible value, this next coin more than makes up for it.

Both coins contain 0.9675oz of gold. Both are close to 100-years old. Both are authentic coins, verified by the highly regarded PCGS.

The difference is, this next coin carries a rating of MS65+. MS means "Mint Standard." It's a rating scale developed by coin grading services to rank coins based on several factors. MS70 means perfect, or virtually untouched.

It's almost impossible to find an old coin rated MS70. The MS65+ rating on the coin pictured below is very high. The additional "+" means the coin rated nicer than MS65 but not quite MS66. That gives it an additional ~$750 of value. Combined with the gold content, that's around $2,400 today.

1928 MS65+ rated coin worth ~$750 more than its gold Content

The coin does not need to be perfect to rate high. Graders look at wear on the edge of the coin. They tend to assign more value for a natural patina covering Lady Liberty for instance.

The Saint-Gaudens is a gold alloy. At 90% gold 10% copper, the mixed metal alloy can over time produce a unique patina.

Rarity is a big part of coin values. There were more than eight million Saints minted in 1928. An estimated 745,000 survived melting. Of those, only 67,500 graded better than MS65. The coin pictured with its MS65+ grading is one of them.

The MS65+ was a great find. It more than made up for the cleaned coin. Averaged together it was still a good buy.

If you focus on one particular type of coin, you'll notice these types of details over time. When you spot them in a coin for sale at a fair price, you could end up with a great deal.

Gold Content + Rarity

I got very interested in coins almost twenty years ago. A close friend bought several Saints every month when gold was around $300-$400/oz. That was back in 2003-2004. Nobody really cared much about coins then.

My friend told me the value of collectible coins shot up far more than gold itself in the 1970s. He thought that might happen again if gold took off. He was right. We might be on the cusp of a similar situation today. The chart below shows gold looks set to take out its all-time high price of 2011. That was a time when collectable coins did very well.

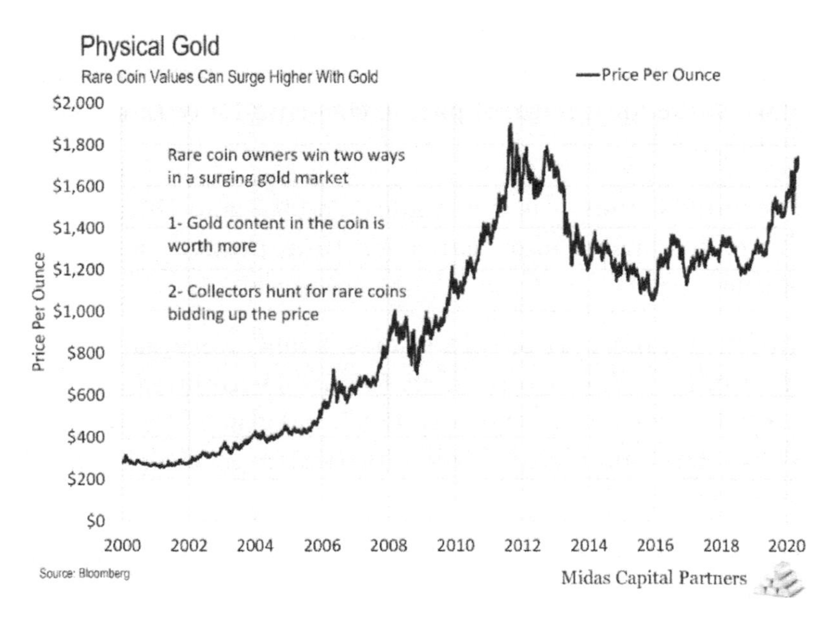

My collector friend taught me the two factors that make up a coin's value. As I said before, one is gold content. That's the easy one. The second is rarity. Rarity also includes the coin's condition.

As for gold content, the 1924 and the 1928 Saints pictured previously cost me about $1,250 each three years ago. Both sat in a tray with other random coins at a local jewelry shop. Neither carried a rating at the time. Consequently, they had no collectible value either.

Gold traded for around $1,225/oz in the spring of 2017. Paying $1,250 for each coin meant a roughly $65 premium over the actual value of the gold content in the Saint. Remember, there's just less than a full troy ounce in each coin.

That means the rarity cost only $65. That turned out to be a deal for the 1928 coin that rated very high at the coin grading service. The 1924 coin on the other hand was a wash. With no collectible value, it only has gold value.

PCGS grades coins and places them in sealed plastic holders with a barcode and hologram. The company requires an annual membership to use its services. However, you can browse the company's extensive database of coin information for free at pcgs.com/coinfacts.

If you have a collection of rare coins sitting in a drawer, consider having them graded. Once graded, coins command more accurate values at auction. That could mean more money staying in your estate instead of being spotted as orphaned coins in a jewelry store by a coin collector with years of experience.

That said, most people should stay out of the collectible coin game. As the price of gold takes off slick salesmen and scammers will flock to the rare coin market. Buyer beware.

Chapter 22 – Gold in Your Brokerage Account

"Where am I going to put all this stuff?"

This always comes up. Over the years I must have fielded this question from clients and shareholders hundreds of times.

If you're just starting out in life, it's not hard to store a modest amount of gold. A dozen coins were worth over $20,000 as of mid-2020. Stacked up they don't take up more than 1.5" of space. A drawer, safe deposit box, wall safe or any secure cranny will do.

Some people have a more serious storage problem. One client bought a gun safe made for shotguns and rifles. That worked for a while. The problems only grow from there.

I had dinner early this year with a gold investor so wealthy he pays a vaulted storage company to guard it. Worse, he had the gold in Asia and had to relocate it to Europe once.

While governments and central banks have unlimited storage options, individuals and corporations don't. You have to consider storage.

Paranoid types might cut a hole in the drywall behind a painting. Wall studs are 16" apart in a standard home. Fashion a little shelf and stack the gold up. Repair the drywall, repaint, and you'll probably die of old age before someone finds it.

The most paranoid might bury gold. An old friend calls this "midnight gardening." I don't recommend it.

Spread your gold out. The bank, a safe, another safe, and a place nobody would think to look. That's the best you can do. Remember, it's wealth insurance you hope you don't need.

Once you've maxed out your capacity for physical gold, there's an easy way to add more without adding headaches. I'm talking about the New York Stock Exchange.

Between 1.5-2% of all the known gold in the world sits in vaults leased by physical gold ETFs. That's exchanged-traded funds set up for the sole purpose of buying gold. There are several. However, they're not all the same. There are two general types. One has the gold, the other doesn't.

Have's and Have Not's

There's not much point in buying physical gold if you can't access it.

I know this might sound obvious, but not all of the physical gold ETFs have actual gold. A few do. The others trade gold futures representing a claim on gold. The two are not the same.

Futures trade on a futures exchange. They exist for most major commodities. The origin of futures makes a lot of sense. Using them to buy gold does not.

Say a farmer produces 10,000 bushels of corn in the fall. Corn sells for $4 per bushel. He can pre-sell his 10,000 bushels of corn for maybe $3.80 today. A speculator enters into a contract for the farmer's future production paying him $3.80 per bushel ($38,000 total) today in exchange for delivery of the actual corn in the fall.

This $38,000 payment gives the farmer badly needed cash to plant, pay workers, and take care of his farm. If the price of corn falls in half, he makes out like a bandit. He doesn't owe the speculator anything other than the physical corn. However, if the price of corn shoots up to $5/bushel, the speculator pockets the difference as he's able to sell the corn for $5/bushel when delivered earning a $12,000 profit.

It's important to understand how futures work to fully grasp why they are not right for gold investors. They might be OK for gold speculators, but even that doesn't make sense once you see other options available.

The largest U.S.-based gold ETF is SPDR Gold Shares (GLD). If you ask your wealth advisor to buy gold, he may suggest this ETF. GLD is the largest exchange-traded fund offering exposure to gold. It trades at high volume averaging over $2 billion per day in the first half of 2020. For big fund managers, it's a good option.

However, holding GLD shares does not entitle you to physical gold. The fund has gold in storage, but you can't have it. Worse, it may use gold futures contracts at times to maintain its gold exposure. And, it might have a claim on gold from a pool with other claimants.

GLD is a $60 billion fund. It's totally above board. But it deals in what we'll call "paper gold."

Another paper gold fund is iShares Gold Trust (IAU). This fund holds almost $24 billion worth of paper gold. It's another good option for funds. But again, there's no way to access the gold for shareholders.

The most popular gold ETFs don't offer physical gold. That means even if you owned $10 million worth of them, you can't get your hands on the physical gold they hold.

At Least Have the Option

There are ETFs that offer physical gold delivery. If the price is the same, it's only logical that these ETFs are more attractive than the most popular Wall Street products.

Sprott Physical Gold and Silver Trust (CEF) offers delivery of physical metal. I do not recommend buying up shares of CEF then calling on the fund to deliver gold. It's cumbersome and could have tax implications. The point is, CEF has the gold (and silver too).

I've been to the CEF corporate headquarters in Toronto several times. I've met with corporate management. They're gold people. Offering delivery of gold held by the fund is important to them.

As a consequence, CEF is smaller than the big New York paper gold funds. CEF's market capitalization is only $3 billion, or one-twentieth the size of GLD. $3 billion is plenty big. Plus, it has the metal.

I'd be shocked if size holds CEF back as gold takes off. In fact, it's more likely there comes a day where its physical gold hoard earns a premium in the market.

Turmoil in the gold market hit an extreme in the first half of 2020. In the first instance I've seen, physical gold and paper gold sold for widely different prices.

As a reminder, paper gold is a futures contract, certificate or some contractual claim on gold ounces. That's a portion of what some of the most popular ETFs hold.

Physical gold means tangible metal held in vaults. That's what Sprott Physical Gold and Silver Trust (CEF) holds.

The next chart explains why holding physical gold matters. For years, nobody thinks about the difference between paper and physical. Then when turmoil hits, the cost of the real thing surges.

By Morgan Stanley's measure, physical gold traded for $50/oz more than paper gold in the market turmoil of spring 2020.

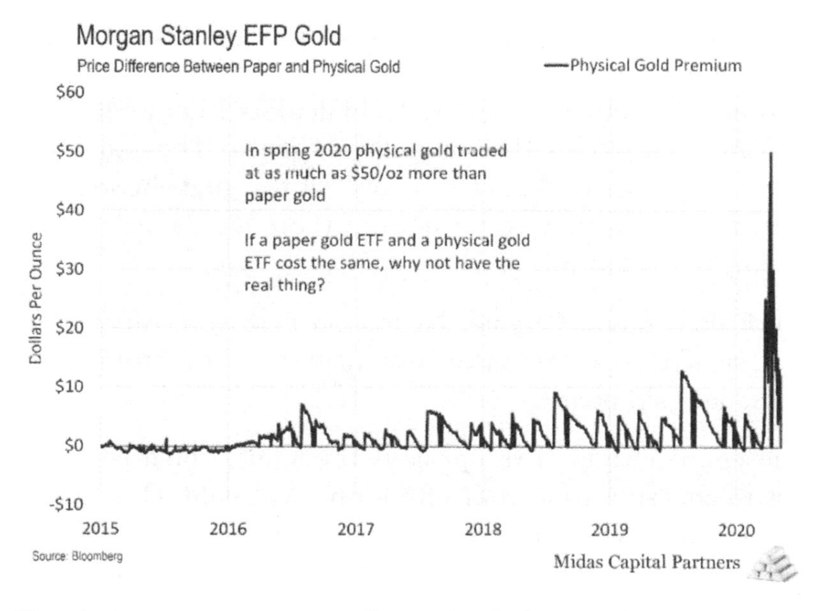

That's just one measure. I watched the gap between New York gold futures traded on the COMEX and physical gold on the London market surge to $80/oz in early April.

The bottom line here is, if the real thing costs the same price, don't mess around with paper.

In addition to the Sprott Trust there's a smaller U.S.-based fund run by long-time gold investor Axel Merk. His fund is VanEck Merk Gold Trust (OUNZ).

Merk's trust is very small clocking in at $250 million market capitalization. It trades about $2.75 million in volume per day. However, it offers delivery in smaller denominations than Sprott.

During the early April 2020 shock to the paper versus physical gold market, Merk put out a press release stating his fund stood ready to deliver.

The April shock is important. While Morgan Stanley only measured $50/oz between paper and physical gold, I witnessed as much as $80/oz. Gold dealers I know charged $150/oz more than the quoted gold price. They told me personally they could not possibly get the gold cheaper. In fact, for weeks they could not get their hands on a fresh supply of gold at all.

Merk does have the gold. He'll send it to you. Again, I'm not sure that's the most practical way to build your personal gold hoard.

The point here is, if the price is the same, you'd be crazy not to choose a fund that offers physical gold. One day it will matter. When that day comes, it's too late to switch.

Chapter 23 – The Extreme Ups and Downs of Mining Stocks

How would you like to have your hard-earned savings tied up in this stock?

This company is still in business today

This chart shows the performance of a real company. Its shares trade today, and it would love for you to buy them. You won't get the stock symbol from me.

Think about the moves on that chart for a moment. They really happened. To see what this is like let's say you invested $10,000 before 2006, the first move, and did not buy or sell any stock through the ups and downs.

The first move sent shares up 4,021% which turned your $10,000 into $412,000 in just 16 months. Not bad. You would definitely think you're a genius at that point.

Just when you thought you had the market figured out, the stock craters, falling 96% in just 20 months. Your initial stake, now valued at $16,480, is still worth 65% more than when you started. That's good. But watching $395,000 evaporate probably wasn't easy.

Good thing you didn't sell, as the stock ran 1,853% over the next few years. That puts you back at $321,850. Maybe now is a good time to get out.

Hopefully you sold. The stock fell 98% in the next two years turning your stake back into $6,437.

This is a real stock. If you attend a mining investment conference today the company likely has a booth. Stop by. It would love to give you a free pen with its logo on it along with a quick sales pitch. You'll hear about how optimistic it is, there's a promising drill result coming, can't talk too much about it.... Sounds like a great story the first time you hear it.

Here's what you don't know.

Mark Twain Had It Right

A mine is a, "Hole in the ground owned by a liar." That's how Mark Twain put it.

He was pretty close. There are some admirable miners. I know a few of them. There could be one or two more I haven't met.

Just before the 98% decline in the mining company stock we just saw, my business partner Brett Heath and I went to Mexico to visit one of the company's projects. We never made it to the site.

Years ago, Brett and I started an asset management firm focused on up-and-coming gold or silver mining stocks. We found there was no competent asset manager focused on up and comers. So, we started one.

We traveled extensively to see the projects we owned shares in. Our clients deserved that, at least that's how we saw it.

The CEO of this company was slick. We knew that going in. Even accounting for his slippery ways, we thought he had the chance to create a major mining firm.

At the time, he had one asset going into production. This means a big investment went into setting up the mining plan and infrastructure. That's usually not the best reason to own a mining stock.

It was the company's other North American asset that had the potential to send the stock sky high. That project was nothing more than scrubland at the time. However, early indications showed potential for a giant mine.

This is what makes mining stocks go boom. Finding and proving the ounces in the ground sends tiny stocks flying higher. Forget about all the future work required to bring the project online. It's the stock surge people want.

There's nothing like a 4,000% gain. Have one, and you'll spend the rest of your life trying to find another one. Try not to go broke in the process.

All Alone in Mexico City

Brett and I traveled on a shoestring budget. We had millions of dollars under management, but in the asset management business that's nothing. When we decided to visit a mine, it was an investment of valuable time and money.

This company invited us hoping after we saw its projects firsthand, we'd buy more stock. We'd been in Mexico for about ten days and this was one of our last companies to visit.

After breakfast we went down to the lobby to wait for our ride. It's customary for the mining firm to send someone for you. For starters, you don't know where you're going. Mexico City is absolutely enormous. It has more residents than New York. Two gringos sitting in traffic is a big waste of time.

An hour passed, no ride. Then another hour. We get a call from the CEO. He tells us we should get a taxi to the bus terminal. Take a four-hour bus ride to a village. Then he'll have someone meet us. No thanks.

It was the beginning of the end for the CEO and his share price. We found out months later he was negotiating a desperation loan to keep the company afloat. Most of that money went to keep himself floating. He defaulted on the loan two weeks after receiving proceeds. Think about that, two weeks. It's worse than failing to make your first mortgage payment.

After all that, the company is still in business today. Its stock ran up 137% in the spring of 2020. It will probably run more. Even junk floats when the tide rises. It's in your best interest I don't tell you the ticker symbol.

A $35 Million Hole in The Ground

One big gain in a mining stock and you'll die trying to get another one.

Mining is a terrible business. It's labor intensive. It requires billions of dollars in capital expenditures. Gold is almost always buried in the world's most remote locations. Then there's Mark Twain's observation.

However, when gold takes off, mining stocks tend to fly higher. Exploration companies can do even better. They don't have a mine. They hunt for the next big discovery. By my estimate 99% of them fail. The 1% that succeed is all people remember.

These are terrible odds. You'd never spin a roulette wheel with 1% odds on your side. People do this again and again with the mining business.

I'm not talking about major mining companies like Barrick Gold (GOLD), Agnico Eagle Mines (AEM), Kinross Gold (KGC), Newmont Corp. (NEM), or AngloGold Ashanti (AU). These firms operate with a high degree of discipline. It shows.

Stocks of these five firms, called "majors," are up on average 113% over the last year. That compares to a 36% rise in gold over the same period. It means these large firms mining gold tripled the return of holding gold itself.

While 113% is the average return for the five majors I mentioned, some did far better individually. AngloGold

Ashanti lead the pack -- up 133% while Agnico Eagle Mines was up "only" 63%. Wise investors pick a handful of stocks and avoid going all-in on what they think will be the one winner.

You'd think 113% in a year is good enough to satisfy investors. Not in this business. They need more. Most of them will lose big trying to find it.

Take the $35 million hole in the ground we saw one time as an example. Today it's full of rainwater.

Brett and I visited this mine site, also in Mexico, several years ago. The company didn't have enough money to fly someone down to meet us. They left us with the indigenous staff, which turned out to be a stroke of luck. These guys told us all the gory details about what happened to the $35 million.

It took forever to get to the site. We flew a Cessna 208 Caravan across the Sea of Cortez. We stayed in a rundown beachfront hotel outside of town. The next day we drove five hours in a truck to what I can confidently tell you is the middle of nowhere.

On site, the local staff was happy to see us. These guys live in the camp. They're supposed to be drilling, cataloging core samples, and supervising the development plan. That was all at a standstill.

All we saw was a big hole in the ground filled with rainwater. Years prior, a major mining firm pulled several hundred thousand ounces of gold from the hole. This smaller firm acquired the property hoping to start things back up.

$35 million down the drain

They figured there had to be more gold in that hole. They took the story to market. Investors liked the plan. They poured a cumulative $35 million into the stock through private placements.

Keep in mind, gold took off in late 2008. It ran 171% in under three years topping out in September 2011. This created a speculative frenzy.

With gold on a run, large mining firms did very well. As the price rises, they make more money. Sell 100,000 ounces of gold for $100/oz more this year compared to last year and it means an extra $10 million in income. Gold ran $1,200 during the 2008-2011 period meaning miners raked in huge profits.

Investors perked up and started looking for the next big gold mine. They financed almost anything with the word gold in the name. They mostly poured money down empty holes in the middle of nowhere.

The stock price of the empty hole we visited shot up 9,300% as the market caught gold fever. It crashed 91% in the following two years as shown in the next chart.

The local mining staff told us about the waste.

They said the company executives formed their own private drilling company. They subcontracted work from the public company at higher than usual prices. They hired private Spanish tutors to help them assimilate. Workers told us this was mostly to help them meet girls in town.

Good food, comfortable lodging, lots of first-class travel to international conferences. Oh, and helicopter service between the airport and the site for executives. That five-hour truck ride mostly on dirt roads was too much to endure.

These guys spent all $35 million. In the end, they had a flooded hole in the ground. We called it an expensive, manmade lake.

If you called it fraud, I wouldn't hold it against you.

The crazy thing is, this stock still trades today. It changed names, more than once. In the last year as gold took off it's up 350%. It will probably run more before finding gravity and finishing where it started.

Lower the Investment Risks of Mining Stocks

If gold takes off to new highs, mining stocks could see an epic surge.

Try to resist the urge to speculate. Yes, there will be huge winners. You'll read stories about them in the financial news. But there will also be lots of heartburn.

Instead of looking for the next 5,000% winner and hoping it will change your life, take the easier way by owning the big, stable mining firms. The five listed earlier are good candidates on the front end of this gold bull market.

Companies pulling gold from the ground should see surging profits as the price of gold moves. If costs are $1,200/oz and you plan for $1,500/oz gold prices, $1,700/oz is a tremendous surprise. If most of that extra $200/oz doesn't flow to the bottom line, there's a problem.

Stick with the winners. The gold business is dangerous. It's been that way for centuries. It won't change anytime soon.

While the profit-making potential of major gold mining firms during a gold bull market sounds exciting, there's one business that puts it to shame. In my experience, it's the most profitable business in the world.

Chapter 24 – The Most Profitable Business in the World

$2 million in and $1 billion out....

That's 500-times the initial investment. Those are real numbers, audited, and owned by shareholders of what I call, "the world's most profitable business."

There could be a company more profitable than Franco-Nevada Corp (FNV), I just haven't found it yet.

Franco is the leading gold royalty company. "Royalty" is what you'd expect kings and queens to own. There's no dirty work involved. It's a straight 1% or 2% right off the top. If 100 ounces of gold come out of the ground, the royalty owner gets one of those ounces at no cost outside of the initial price paid for the royalty. Think of it like a tax. In this case, you're the taxman.

In the mid-1980s the two men who put Franco-Nevada together came to the same conclusion I shared with you in the previous chapter. Hunting for the next great gold mine is a racket. You might get lucky and actually find something. You might get a lift generally during a gold bull market. But you'll need some sort of happy accident or else you're bankrupt every few years.

Franco talked about the idea of buying a few royalty claims to generate income. This steady cash flow coming in the door would keep the company afloat. One of the founders mentioned it to consultants helping the company in 1985.

A few months later, one of the consultants called up and asked if Franco would pay him a finder's fee for a tip on a royalty for sale. They agreed. The consultant produced a copy of a classified ad from a local Nevada newspaper advertising a royalty for sale.

Franco paid $2 million for the royalty. It paid the consultant $90,000 for producing the newspaper.

The royalty covered 3,416 acres of dusty land in Northeastern Nevada. Elko is the closest major town about one hour east. A Texas-based oil company owned the royalty but had to sell it due to financial trouble.

West of Elko, several companies found gold known as "Carlin-type." This is a lower-grade deposit where it's almost hard to see the gold. There were clusters of similar finds in the area. Carlin-type gold deposits can be much larger than other types. That's what was under the ground on Franco's new royalty claim.

Owning a royalty means a mining company hunts for gold on the property where you have a claim to a small part of every ounce found. Once production begins, 1% or 2% of everything produced flows directly to the royalty holder. The royalty company doesn't do any digging, exploring or much of anything after acquiring the initial royalty interest.

Within months of purchasing the royalty west of Elko, Franco got lucky. The mining company working on its claim discovered what's to this day one of the richest

Carlin-type gold deposit in the world producing in excess of 45 million ounces of gold to date. It's still in production today.

That $2 million royalty will pay back over $1 billion. It still pays today.

Franco hasn't paid a cent to dig, blast, haul, process, or transport the gold. Just as you'd expect from a king or queen, it takes delivery of its percentage payment right on time like clockwork from the comfort of its Toronto offices.

$27 Billion with 26 People

Franco has over $1 billion in market value for each employee. I don't know any company that comes close.

Apple has only $13 million in market value per employee. Microsoft has only $9.7 million. Google has only $7.7 million. Ecommerce giant Amazon has a paltry $1.4 million of market value per employee.

The royalty business is the most lucrative I know of and Franco is its blue-chip leader. It has hundreds of royalties today. It's a very big company. But only employs 26 people.

Company	Market Cap	Employees	Market Cap Per Employee
FNV	**$26,949,500,000**	**26**	**$1,036,519,231**
APPLE	$1,336,600,000,000	100,000	$13,366,000
MSFT	$1,401,200,000,000	144,000	$9,730,556
GOOG	$943,505,400,000	123,048	$7,667,783
AMZN	$1,194,500,000,000	840,400	$1,421,347

**values as of May 2020 in $USD*

The Value of "Optionality"

The secret to the royalty business is "optionality." That means buying something with unlimited potential and minimal effort required on your part to realize it. There are not many things in life that meet this definition. Royalties are one of them. If bought properly of course.

Take Franco's $2 million royalty west of Elko for example. I highly doubt the company knew how successful that royalty would become. They knew there was Carlin gold in the area. They knew there was activity on the property, meaning active exploration for gold. But there's no way they knew how good it would be.

The trick is to buy royalties near known gold deposits. Gold tends to show up in clusters. If there's a good find in an area, it's probably not the only one. You want a royalty next to that find. And you don't want to pay much for it. You never know which royalty will pay off. The best companies gather up as many of them as possible betting one of them will hit.

What was a smaller deposit at the time later became one of the largest gold mines in North America. Called Goldstrike, a large mining company discovered it on Franco's new property. As a reminder, everything found on a royalty claim falls under the claim owner's right to 1% or 2%, or whatever the terms dictate.

Once the mining company found more gold, it expanded work on the site. It's been doing that for 30 years. Goldstrike is so big you can see the hole in the ground from satellite images.

With hundreds of royalty claims spread across the world, Franco still values optionality. It's not the expensive high-profile royalties that make a company. It's the low-cost royalty near a previous gold discovery that has the power to turn $2 million into $1 billion.

Investors who bought Franco stock in the 1983 IPO did very well. In his book Get Smarter, one of the founders, Seymour Schulich, said $1,000 invested in the 1983 IPO turned into $1.25 million by early 2004 when Newmont acquired the company. That's 1,250-times your money while other mining companies do all the hard work.

Franco came back to the public markets in late 2007. Since that time, the price of gold is up 111% and Franco's stock is up 823% not including dividends. (We're using the company's U.S. listing priced in dollars. It has a primary listing in Canada.)

Gold royalties are the best bet on higher gold prices I know of, as the next chart shows. It tracks royalty industry leader Franco-Nevada's shares from its most recent IPO in late 2007.

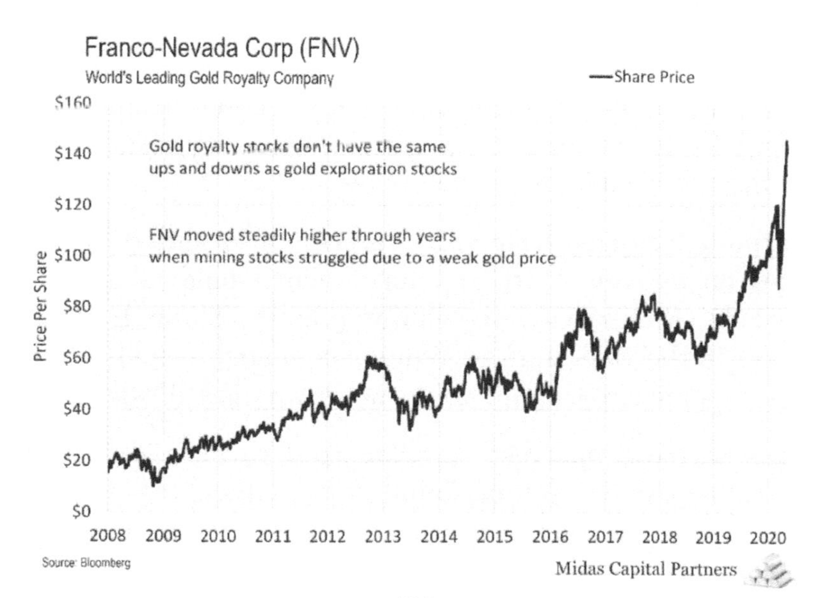

Naysayers complain about royalty stocks. They say the stocks are too expensive. They say you miss out on the exciting potential for a huge gold discovery. They're right on both counts.

Royalty stocks are expensive. As with most things in life, you get what you pay for. A $0.10/share mining stock with the chance at a big discovery only needs your money to roll the dice. With 99 out of 100 failing to produce anything other than mounting losses, the risk on the $0.10/share stock is high. I say that makes it more expensive than the royalty stock.

Perpetual Claim

The Franco founders started out on the other side of the business looking for gold.

They realized they'd have to sell stock endlessly to finance gold exploration. Over time that would dilute the value of their stock. If they ever did find something, they'd own a smaller piece of it. That's why they shifted to the royalty business.

A royalty claim represents a perpetual, non-dilutable, free carried interest in a mineral asset. Once you acquire the claim, there's not much ongoing work.

Perpetual means the royalty interest in a mineral claim goes on forever. Most are permanent, some cover time periods. Either way, the claim remains through tough years in the gold market. When a company picks back up and resumes looking for gold, the royalty is still there.

Free carried interest means the royalty covers a percentage of everything found in the future. It's "free" in that it does not require the royalty holder to help finance development or operational expenses.

Projects tend to keep growing. Once the company is a mile underground, it usually keeps looking for more gold. Royalty claims cover everything found on the property.

My Money's on Gold Royalties

There are only six pure-play royalty companies today. That's my count, and excludes smaller and still unproven companies, or those that dabble in mining.

My business partner Brett Heath and I learned a lot managing a gold mining stock fund. The most important thing we learned was mining is a terrible business.

Again and again we'd noticed small footnotes in mining company financial reports. Some LLC or private individuals received a small payment monthly or quarterly tied to production. This was a royalty not owned by Franco-Nevada or the other large companies.

Brett came up with an idea. There must be thousands of these orphaned royalties. Many of them cover ground owned by major mining companies. He figured at least a few of these individual owners would sell to him.

Here's where the pitch shifted. Brett figured anybody can open up a big checkbook and make an offer for the royalty. That's passé, and cheap considering the powerful nature of royalties.

He told these owners the value of their royalty individually was too low. They deserved more. Selling to him, in exchange for stock, would not only get them fair value, over time they'd get a premium.

The ones who listened to him early made a fortune. His company, Metalla Royalty & Streaming (MTA) came public at a split-adjusted $0.80/share in late 2016. As the next chart shows, MTA traded for more than $6/share just 40 months later. That does not include cash dividends, paid monthly by the company and tied to 50% of its operating cash flow.

To be clear, Metalla was not a “sweetheart deal” available to only the most connected. A decade of business interests and friendship didn’t yield me any special treatment. Anyone had the chance to get into Metalla in late 2016. I even presented on the topic at the Sprott Resource Conference in Vancouver months in advance. Some people took action and still hold shares today.

Having been in business with Brett through challenging times and fully understanding the power of the royalty business, I bought stock hand over fist in the open market. I kept that up for 40 months. Each time the stock rose, it seemed like it didn’t rise enough to meet what I felt was fair value.

About two months into operation Brett asked me to join the board of directors. I gladly accepted.

Sitting on the board of a public company carries an important responsibility. Directors represent shareholders. They should set the course for the company with that in mind. Then, they should get out of the way and let management work.

Brett is the industry's most talented dealmaker. He's excruciatingly detailed when it comes to setting up a royalty deal. As of publication, he's done it 17 times buying 48 royalty interests.

Royalties are not easy to acquire. There's no website listing them for sale like real estate. The best deals start out as relationships.

Brett figured out the trick to creating maximum shareholder value in a royalty company is:

- Acquire royalties of a similar size – You don't want one giant royalty and fifty small ones

- Avoid paying up for immediate production – The value is in optionality, as Franco-Nevada demonstrated with its $2 million Nevada royalty purchase

- Go cheap on dangerous regions – If the mine is in a warzone, bid accordingly

- Avoid small producers – The majors pay their bills, the smaller firms run out of money forcing you into court

- Acquire optionality – Buy as many royalty claims near proven production zones as you can get your hands on and pay as little as possible knowing one will eventually hit pay dirt

A Firsthand Example of This

In April 2020, Metalla announced a royalty transaction that checked all of these boxes.

Located about one hour southeast of Franco's billion-dollar royalty, it has similar potential. Metalla picked up royalties covering a large swath of land. The trick here is, its royalty claims border a multi-million-ounce mining operation as the map shows.

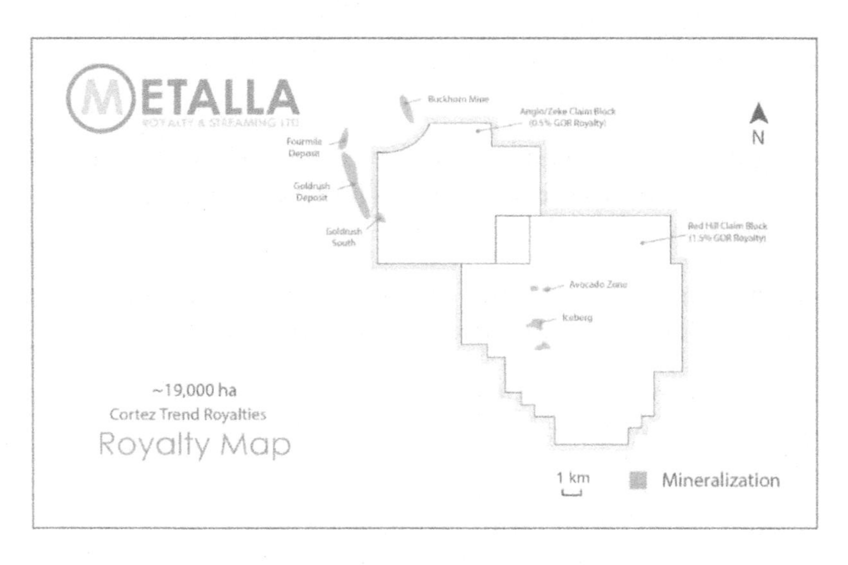

MTA claims (outlined) sit adjacent to known gold mineralization

This is optionality. Metalla sits and waits to see if the $46 billion mining company next door finds more gold on its claim. It paid $4 million for the package of claims. Time will tell their true value.

Chapter 25 – Summing It All Up

Throughout this book we laid the framework for what could be the most dramatic gold rally in modern history. In fact, it may go down as the most dramatic rally of any asset class.

Gold is money, in a time when money has lost its way.

The value of all the gold in the world is a fraction of the piles of debt, mountains of financial derivatives, and surging liabilities holding back the economy today. As the world's financial system barrels towards an inevitable reset, gold may be the only asset that holds value.

We know the importance of owning physical gold. At least a good portion of this should be stored safely outside of the financial markets. That means not traded on an exchange or held by an unknown custodian. There's no substitute for real, hold in your hand gold.

As the size of your gold hoard grows, you may need to own some gold on an exchange or held with a broker. But physical gold in and of itself is not an investment. It's wealth insurance.

As the cracks in the financial system show, gold maintains its value. Through the Great Depression, gold held its value. Remember, during economic turmoil, your goal is to suffer less than the average person. Gold makes that possible.

At the same time, gold mining stocks thrived. The cost of operating mines fell during the Depression years. Labor, energy, and materials all grew cheaper while the value of gold did not.

The government fixed the price of gold in those days. Today it floats freely. Nations, central banks, and wealthy families all move to gold during times of trouble. Speculators will follow. The problem is, there's not enough gold to meet that increased demand.

As the price takes off, your physical gold goes up in value. Already today, the price of physical gold coins runs as high as $200/oz more than the price of gold quoted on the London exchange. That means only one thing: demand for physical gold is high.

It's important to position in gold before it goes mainstream. The gold rally will only happen once. That means, once gold takes off, there's no going back. Once you hear about it every day in the financial media, it's too late.

A major gold rally will be good for physical gold holders; it could be life changing for speculators.

With physical gold safely stored, it's time to speculate. Here are the speculative segments of the gold industry in order of risk from lowest to highest:

- Royalty Companies
- Major Producers
- Mid-tier Producers

- Junior Producers
- Development Companies
- Exploration Companies

After two decades in the gold sector I rarely touch exploration companies. There's the odd occasion a friend raises money and I make a small investment. Generally, I see these as a very bad use of hard-earned savings.

If you can't resist, keep exploration company investments small. Since you're playing for a big surprise outcome, bet accordingly. $1,000 into the original Franco-Nevada turned into $1.25 million. Exploration stock buyers usually aren't so lucky.

That's why I've made a serious bet on gold royalties.

However, nothing lasts forever. There will be a day to sell winning royalty stocks, major mining companies, and possibly even physical gold itself. While that day is not today, it's important to know how to spot it.

Chapter 26 – When to Sell

It's important to remember that investing in gold stocks is not a forever trade. Everything has its season. There will be a time to sell gold stocks. There may even be a time to sell physical gold itself.

Throughout my career, when to sell is the one question that always makes me laugh. People want certainty more than anything else. They think someone has the answers in advance. They never figure out that nobody has the answers.

The best decision makers in the money game never look outside for the answers, only the clues. Once they see the clues, the decision is easy to make. Unfortunately, knowing when to sell is more feeling than science.

Some Indicators I Use

I'd like to leave you with some of the indicators I'll use to determine when gold is too rich.

The first is the Dow Gold Ratio.

Pierre Lassonde, former Chairman of Franco-Nevada, came up with the Dow Gold ratio in an FNV annual report to shareholders around 20 years ago. At the time, gold seemed cheap. He wanted to show people how cheap. He was right.

Lassonde calculated how many gold ounces you could buy with one share of the Dow Jones Industrial Average. At the time, gold sold for under $300/oz. The Dow traded over 11,000. That put the Dow Gold Ratio over 36. It ran as high as 45 briefly in August 1999.

He then explained that when that ratio reached high levels, it meant gold was too cheap. When it fell to the low single-digits, gold was expensive. The next chart shows how this looks over time.

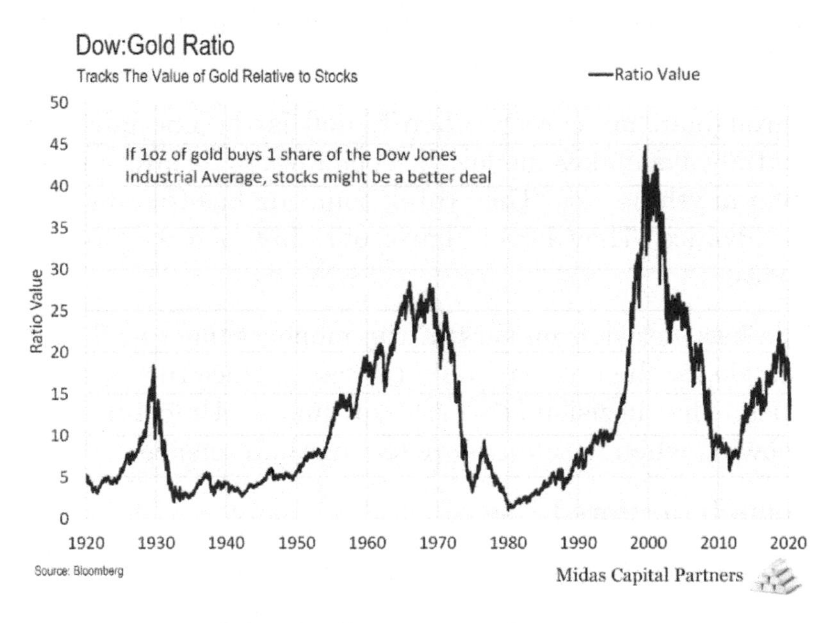

Good indicator of gold's value

Today the ratio reads just over 14. It could fall much lower.

For perspective, 1:1 would put the gold price even with the Dow. Imagine gold at $5,000/oz and the Dow Jones

Industrial Average at 5,000. That would be an extreme. A ratio of 2:1 could be gold $5,000/oz: Dow 10,000.

There's no exact number to watch for in the ratio. When it gets low, very low, it's time to start thinking about making a move.

Again, this ratio will help you spot extremes in both directions. When it read over 40, gold was so cheap almost no one wanted it. Gold went on to rise 643% over the next decade. That high reading on the Dow Gold Ratio marked an extreme low point for gold.

A low reading of the ratio would likely mark another extreme. This time, on the opposite side. If gold and the Dow traded for the same price, a 1:1 ratio, stocks would be so cheap people might think they'd go away forever. If you see this, it's time to at least consider what you can buy with the proceeds from selling gold.

Compare Gold to Other Assets

Assets are only valuable relative to other assets. That means if stocks doubled in value and real estate stayed flat, you could sell your portfolio and buy twice as much real estate. That would be a time to consider such a move.

The most successful investors I know don't worry about what they paid for an asset. They only care what it's worth.

You hear novice traders do just the opposite all the time. "I'll sell when I have a 20% gain." People say this as if their performance has some bearing on which way the market moves. Your purchase price has nothing to do with what's next for the stock price.

When I sold my largest stock holding Lincoln National (LNC) in early September 2008 I spared myself from a 90%

decline. However, LNC was about 25% lower when I sold than earlier that year. If I watched my cost and not the overall market, I might have held on. That would have been an expensive mistake.

Pay attention to what you see in front of you, not the past.

I expect the price of gold to surge as other assets disappoint their owners. Commercial real estate values rely on paying tenants. The same goes for apartments and other rentals. When people struggle to pay rent, the value of the building drops. When there's a loan on the property, trouble spreads.

Gold depends on no other party for its value. Nobody has to pay rent, show up, or do anything. Gold's only serious threat is theft. That's typically preventable.

If the value of gold shines and other assets falter, pay attention to sentiment. This is as easy as listening to what people say about each.

When I bought rental houses for $0.10 on the dollar in 2009-2010 people were very negative. They'd ask what I was up to, hoping to get an investment tip. I'd say, "buying real estate as fast as possible." They'd lecture me on how dangerous real estate was, citing the recent mortgage meltdown.

It wasn't until 2012-2013 that I started hearing people talk positively about real estate again. By 2014-2015 flippers and speculators were back. By the end of the decade rap star Pitbull had conferences pushing hard money loans and quick turn investments in real estate. Time to get out.

Nobody likes gold today, generally speaking. If you start hearing people bragging about gold and gold stocks at cocktail parties, look out. It might be time to reassess the trade.

Asset markets move higher until they run out of buyers. Think back to tech stocks in 1999. At the end of the mania, almost everyone owned at least one of them.

The manager of a country diner in North Carolina wrote down a pink sheet ticker symbol on the back of my receipt in 1999. He told me he wasn't sure what the company did, but the stock was a real bargain. I'll never forget that. It was a sign that things had run their course.

If you see gold making front page news, mainstream television headlines, or getting a lot of positive press, pay close attention. These are the indications something is getting hot. When it gets too hot it's better to start moving away, or at least preparing to.

The final stage of any bull market can be the most violent. In January 1980, the price of gold hit an all-time high of $850/oz. $400 of that came in the last sixty days. That's an extreme. Traders call it a "blow off" marking the top of the market. After that top gold fell for twenty years before kicking off its next run.

Everything has its season. Don't overstay any trade.

Silver as an Indicator

Another indicator I use frequently is the value of gold compared to silver.

Like gold, silver is a precious metal once used as money. Silver coins have similar wealth storage properties.

If you're just starting out, silver coins could be a more practical choice. They're cheap. Today, they're excessively cheap.

The next chart shows how many silver ounces you can buy for one gold ounce.

The 20-year average is 65. That means, on average, you could trade one gold ounce for 65 silver ounces.

Considering the average, a ratio reading above 65 would be more expensive, below 65 less expensive.

Today, it's 110. In March 2020 it reached 125, an extreme no one had ever seen before.

Here's why this matters. Silver is a speculative metal. People tend to gamble on silver more so than gold. Gold is the money of countries and kings. The wealthiest families in the world own gold as wealth insurance.

Silver is difficult to own in large quantities. $8,000 worth of silver fills a size-14 shoebox. $8,000 worth of gold barely fills a shot glass.

Going back to 2000, whenever this ratio reaches an extreme it signals a big rally in gold and gold stocks. If that held true for the extreme reading of 125 in early 2020, it may signal the rally of a lifetime in those assets.

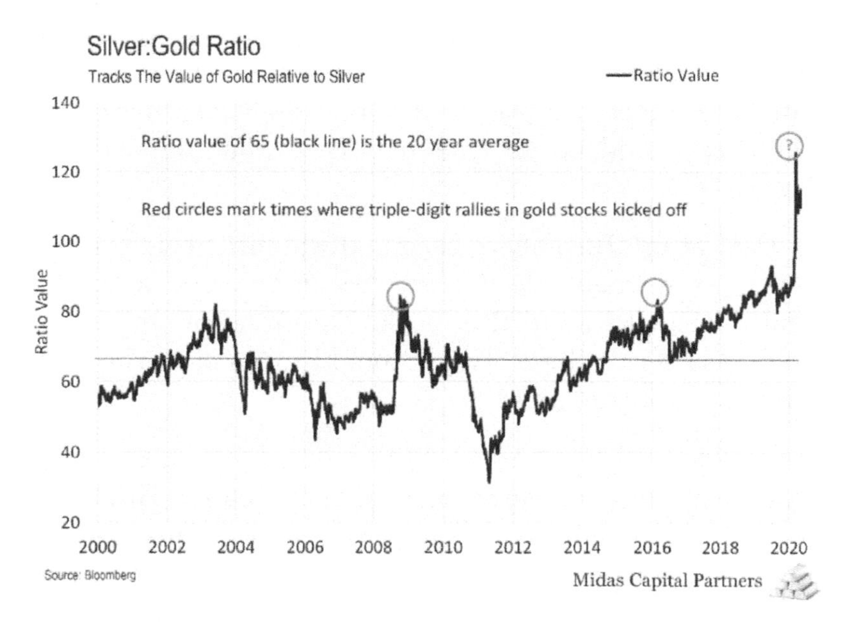

Value of silver ounces to one gold ounce

You can calculate this ratio anytime by dividing the gold price by the silver price. If gold is $2,000 and silver is $50 the ratio would be 40. As you can see in the chart, the last time the ratio hit 40 marked a good time to sell silver and gold, along with the stocks mining each.

At the Threshold of Major Change

I wrote this book during the Covid-19 national shutdown in late spring 2020.

I'd been involved in the gold market for a long time. I'd helped Metalla Royalty (MTA) grow from a penny stock to trading on the New York Stock Exchange. We used the stock to buy close to fifty royalties increasing the company's market value nearly ten-fold during my board tenure.

Up until that point, I thought gold might take out its old highs of $1,900/oz reached in 2011 then add a few hundred more per ounce. Maybe we'd get to $2,500/oz, certainly $3,000/oz would be an extreme. That's out the window now.

As I sat at my Bloomberg terminal watching every major world government flood their economy with stimulus funds, I had to write this book. The first round totaled more than $12 trillion. That's roughly 15% of world GDP printed out of thin air. *Why Gold?*

Meanwhile, stocks cratered. They fell like a rock, and as of May 2020 only recovered part of their losses. However, everyone seemed eager to jump back into the market. To me it looked like 1930 where people went broke trying to pick a bottom the market didn't find for three years.

While stocks fell and didn't fully recover in spring 2020, gold fell and rebounded to a new high. This told me gold was ready to go. *Why Now?*

At the same time, I had friends asking about gold. They knew I spent years focused on the subject. They had no idea how to buy it. Some even thought it was illegal. They needed a handbook to help them through the confusing maze.

When this is over, every broker will tell you gold is a must-own asset. Today they tell you you've lost your mind to have it. That shows how far we have to go.

E.B. Tucker

May 2020

Let's stay connected on:

Made in the USA
Monee, IL
10 October 2020